CW00503254

# Foreword

I am delighted to have this opportunit, _v contribute a foreword
to 'A Paupers' Palace'. It enables me to pay tribute to Betty
Connor, who has spent so much of her time in researching and
writing this book.

I am sure that it will be of great interest to the people of
Bolton and district and to students of the social conditions that
existed between the seventeenth century and the emergence of the
Welfare State in 1948.

I can think of no-one better to have undertaken this task. Not
only did Betty spend her early life within the confines of the
institution, but subsequently she became the Matron of a
residential establishment. Her affection for 'Fishpool' and
'Townleys' can be seen clearly throughout this book.

The reader will find this an absorbing account of the progress
made in the care of the sick and poor, from the days when the
parishes were required to provide the care previously undertaken by the monasteries, to 1948, when the National Health
Service took over responsibility.

Since 1948 there have been many and major developments on the
site. It is now the Bolton District General Hospital, an
institution providing a very high standard of care and treatment - a hospital of which Bolton can be justly proud.

Don Ernsting

# Preface

As a little three-year-old girl I waited with my mother and father outside the big iron gates of the Institution. Soon a porter opened the gates and let us in, to go along the drive to a mass of dark buildings. Although I did not know it then, this was to be my home for more than twenty years. I lived there not as an inmate, but because I was the daughter of the resident Engineer.

After many years away, I returned to the hospital as a voluntary worker. The changes in the care of the elderly and infirm that have taken place are a credit to the various governing bodies and their staffs over the years. In a building that was 'The Workhouse', the wards and departments are beautifully decorated and comfortable; most departments are altered beyond recognition. The exterior structure remains as a monument to those stalwart members of the Bolton Union who fought hard to open such a prestigious, purpose-built establishment for the workless and destitute of all ages in Bolton and its surrounding districts in 1861.

# Contents

The History of Care .. .. .. .. .. .. .. .. .. .. .. .. .. .. .. 5
The Paupers' Palace .. .. .. .. .. .. .. .. .. .. .. .. .. .. .. 7
The Early Years .. .. .. .. .. .. .. .. .. .. .. .. .. .. .. .. 10
Local Government Board Inspections .. .. .. .. .. .. .. .. .. 14
Allegations of Scandal .. .. .. .. .. .. .. .. .. .. .. .. .. 19
Taking on Staff .. .. .. .. .. .. .. .. .. .. .. .. .. .. .. .. 20
Taking Stock; Entertainments .. .. .. .. .. .. .. .. .. .. .. 23
The Royal Commission and Social Changes .. .. .. .. .. .. .. 31
The Great War Years .. .. .. .. .. .. .. .. .. .. .. .. .. .. 39
Post War Changes .. .. .. .. .. .. .. .. .. .. .. .. .. .. .. 43
Segregation and Improvements .. .. .. .. .. .. .. .. .. .. .. 45
Townleys Hospital and Extensions .. .. .. .. .. .. .. .. .. 47
Public Assistance Committee Takes Over .. .. .. .. .. .. .. 52
Modernisation and other changes .. .. .. .. .. .. .. .. .. .. 57
Wartime .. .. .. .. .. .. .. .. .. .. .. .. .. .. .. .. .. .. 63
The Greatest Improvements for the Quality of Life .. .. .. .. 71
Acknowledgements .. .. .. .. .. .. .. .. .. .. .. .. .. .. .. 78

# A PAUPERS' PALACE

## The History of Care

Poor Law dates back to Elizabethan times, when parishes or townships were required by law to provide money from the rates for the relief of the poor. Local overseers were appointed to decide who should qualify for relief, and to distribute the money.

Because poor people became a burden on the rates of any township they moved into, an Act of Settlement was passed in 1662. This empowered township officers to remove strangers within forty days of arrival, unless the newcomers occupied property worth £10 per year. One of the effects of this Act was to make it difficult for people to find work outside their own township. To alleviate this problem, another Act was passed in 1697, permitting township officers to issue a certificate to anyone who wanted to travel to look for employment elsewhere. The certificate carried the township's promise to accept back the person named, and provide for him or her should it become necessary.

Also at this time there was the Apprenticeship Certificate; money was provided from the rates to train pauper children in a job so that they would not be a burden on the township as their parents had been.

Around 1800 the Poor Law was changed to include the provision to pay people in kind, rather than, or as well as, money. This was known as Outdoor Relief. This type of giving was supported by various charities of the township. The Ann Mort Charity in Farnworth, for example, gave lengths of linen cloth to the poor.

A workhouse was built in Fletcher Street, Bolton, in 1810/11. The Bolton Union of 26 townships in and around Bolton was formed in 1837, and in that year two old, small workhouses at Little Hulton and Westhoughton were closed. The inmates were transferred to other, 'better' workhouses at Fletcher Street and at Goose Cote Farm, Turton. There was an early form of work-house in Old Hall Street, Bolton, in premises which later became the Three Arrows public house. Part of the building remains today, now a ladies' toilet.

The teenage boy inmates at Goose Cote were put to work on odd jobs and gardening at Turton Tower. In 1839 the Governor of Goose Cote wanted the boys to take sandwiches to the Tower for their dinner. However, the owner of the residence would not allow them to eat on the premises, so they had to trail back-wards and forwards between the Tower and the workhouse at dinner time.

# R U L E S,

## TO BE OBSERVED IN THE

# W O R K - H O U S E,

### AT TURTON.

<hr/>

**ARTICLE FIRST**

THAT the Mafter and Miftrefs be fober and orderly Perfons, not given to Swear; and that they fee the Orders ftrictly performed.

**II.**

THAT all Perfons, upon their admiffion, deliver up what Houfehold Goods and Cloaths they are poffeffed of to the Mafter, in order to be cleaned and made ufeful for the Service of this Houfe; and if any Perfon fhall conceal any Linen, Woollen, or Houfehold Furniture, with intent to Steal or Embezzle, fuch Perfons fhall immediately be carried before a Magiftrate, in order to be imprifoned and punifhed with the utmoft Rigour, as the Law Directs.

**III.**

THAT Prayers be read in the Houfe every Evening before Supper; and that Grace be faid before and after each Meal; and that all who are able, and do not attend at Prayers, fhall lofe their next Dinner.

**IV.**

THAT all that are able and in Health do go to Church every Sunday; Morning and Afternoon; that they return Home as foon as Divine Service is over; and if any be found loitering or begging by the Way, to lofe their next Meal. And if at any time they get Drunk, or are guilty of prophane Curfing and Swearing, to be punifhed in the ftocks as the Law Directs, and to be debar'd going out during the Mafter's Pleafure.

**V.**

THAT no Perfon fhall prefume to go out of the Street Door without a certain on Leave, and to return in good order at time appointed, upon Pain of being denied going out during the Mafter's Pleafure, and for the fecond Offence to be expelled the Houfe.

**VI.**

THAT no diftilled Liquor or ftrong Drink be brought into the Houfe; and that whofoever fhall difturb the Houfe by brawling, quarreling, fighting, or abufive Language, fhall lofe one Day's Meat, and for the fecond Offence be put in the Dungeon twenty-four Hours.

**VII.**

THAT all Perfons in health do rife in the Morning by five o'clock, and come to work by fix, from Lady Day to Michaelmas; and from Michaelmas to Lady Day, that they rife by fix, and come to work by feven, upon Pain of being kept on Bread and Water, or expelled the Houfe.

**VIII.**

THAT all perfons who through Idlenefs may pretend themfelves fick, lame, or infirm, fo as to be excufed from their Labour, if fuch impofters be difcovered by their Stomachs or by the Phyficians, fhall be carried before a Magiftrate, to be punifhed feverely as the Law Directs.

**IX.**

THAT they go to Bed in the Summer at nine, and in the Winter by eight o'Clock; and, that the Mafter fee all the Candles out.

**X.**

THAT all Provifion be clean and well dreffed; to go to Breakfaft in the Summer at eight, and in the Winter at nine o'clock; Dinner at one all the Year; Supper at fix; to be allowed Half an Hour at Breakfaft, and a whole Hour at Dinner; and all that have not finifhed their Tafk by Supper, to work afterwards 'till finifhed, and great Care taken that they fit decently at Meat.

**XI.**

THAT if any Perfon falls Sick or Lame, Notice to be given to the Apothecary, by the Mafter, with all convenient fpeed, to be taken Care of; and fuch other Victuals be allotted to the Patient befides what is daily ufed, as fhall be thought proper by the Phyfician.

**XII.**

THAT all Beds be made in the Morning by nine, and every Room and Paffage fwept and cleaned by ten o'Clock, and to be wafhed three Times a Week in Summer, and once in Winter; the Difhes to be wafhed twice a Day or oftener; no wafte Fire to be made, and in Summer none at all, except in the Kitchen or Wafh-houfe in Time of Ironing.

**XIII.**

THAT all the Children be wafhed and cleaned by eight o'Clock in the Morning, and fome proper Perfons chofe to teach them to Read.

**XIV.**

THAT the Nurfe take care to make and mend all Linen and Cloaths, and when any Perfon dies, to deliver his other Cloaths to the Mafter, to be laid up in the Wardrobe or Store-room; and alfo every thing elfe they die poffeffed of, for the Ufe of the Houfe.

**XV.**

THAT every Perfon endeavour to preferve Unity, and look upon themfelves as one Family; and to prevent Difputes that may create Difference among themfelves, by forging or telling Lies, fuch Perfon fo offending, on good Proof made thereof, fhall be fet upon a Stool, in the moft public Place in the Dining-Room, whilft at Dinner, and a Paper prefixed upon his or her Breaft, with thefe Words, ( *Infamous Liar*) and likewife to lofe that Meal.

**XVI.**

THAT the School-mafter or Miftrefs fhall teach all the Children, as foon as they are fit to learn, the Church Catechifm.

**XVII.**

THAT no Perfons but a benefactor to this Houfe fhall be allowed to come into any of the Wards, Dining-Room, or Working-Room, without Leave from the Governor; and if any defire to fpeak with any of the Poor, though their neareft Relations, they are not to be allowed without Leave.

**XVIII.**

THAT on the Lord's Day, either before Church or after Dinner, the Mafter do read, or caufe to be read, the Pfalms and Leffons appointed for the Morning Service; and after Evening Prayer, the Pfalms and Leffons appointed for the Evening Service; and alfo a Section or Chapter out of the Whole Duty of Man.

**XIX.**

THAT the Veftry, every Month, or oftener if they fee Caufe, do examine all the Bills and accounts of the Expence of the maintaining the Poor in the Work-houfe; and alfo the accounts of all Materials brought in, or Work done or fold, and obferve the feveral Rates and Prices charged, and give fuch Directions thereupon as they fhall think fit, with regard to the better maintaining and employing the Poor, and faving the Parifh Money.

**XX.**

THAT Care be taken none of the Materials of the feveral Manufactories be wafted or Spoiled, and that there be no defacing of Walls, or breaking of Windows; and that thefe Orders be publicly read every Week, that none may pretend Ignorance.

**XXI.**

THAT the Faults and Diforders of the Poor, whether old or young, who refufe or contemn the Reproofs of the Mafter or Miftrefs; or ufe ill Language againft them, or neglect their Inftructions, be recorded in a Book to be kept for that Purpofe, and laid before the Directors or Overfeers, that by their Authority and Admonition, Rudenefs, Wickednefs, and Difhonefty may be reftrained, and Peace and good Order maintained; and that a Magiftrate be folicited to punifh all obftinate, perverfe, and unruly Perfons, according to their Crimes.

<hr/>

HAWORTH, PRINTER, BURY.

The 1834 Poor Law Act stated that all poor, able-bodied people should be relieved in a workhouse, instead of being allowed money from the rates so that they could stay in their own homes. The supposed effect of this was to make people work harder to keep their own homes; conditions in any workhouse at that time were intended to be much worse and very unpleasant.

Some Unions (the authorities which ran the townships) started to build workhouses as soon as the Act was passed, but Bolton Union decided to carry on with outdoor relief and the small workhouses in Fletcher Street and at Turton.

In January 1856 the Board of Guardians began negotiations to buy land in Farnworth from Cockey Moor Church, Ainsworth. The sale was delayed by the untimely death of the vicar, Rev Carr. He was succeeded by Rev McDonald Evanson, and through him and his officers of the Church the land, known as Fishpool Farm, was eventually purchased in 1858 for £2,880. Foundation stones were laid in the same year.

The main buildings cost £17,753 to erect; the outbuildings and fittings cost a further £6,680. The area occupied by the buildings was eight statute acres, and the tower (which is still a landmark), was built to a height of 72 feet. The architect was George Woodhouse, who also designed Bolton Town Hall.

## The Paupers' Palace

On 28th September 1861, due mainly to the efforts of the Rev Shepherd Birley, an undertaking of the highest importance to the ratepayers of Bolton was completed. John Sheperd Birley MA was Curate of All Saints, Little Bolton, from 1834 to 1843. Later he became Vice President of the Poor Protection Society (which ran soup kitchens and so on) and as a result of that appointment he became a member of the Board of Guardians in 1839.

The Institution was 'superior in workmanship and satisfactory in every minor detail as any Workhouse in the United Kingdom,' according to the Bolton Chronicle of 29th September 1861. Poor people from Bolton and Turton were installed at Fishpool and inmates from Fletcher Street and Goose Cote Farm workhouses were transferred there.

The first Master and Matron at Fishpool were Edward and Lavinia Greenhalgh, who were previously at Fletcher Street Workhouse. (Lavinia was my great-grandfather's cousin.) It would perhaps seem not a good idea to appoint a couple from a deteriorating old workhouse, with old methods. However, it was better to appoint people with some experience of running such an establishment, for at that time there would have been few couples to choose from with the relevant experience. In those early days, the Master was referred to as 'The Guv'nor' by inmates and staff. The first Medical Officer was Dr Robert Alex Clarke of Farnworth.

7

The population of Bolton in 1861 was 130,270, and the number of beds in the workhouse (900) was considered adequate for the needs of the poor and destitute. Males were kept separate from females and children from adults. The adults were divided into two classes - able-bodied and infirm and aged. The children were segregated male and female, seniors and juniors, and placed away from the adults. All departments had separate yards and staircases communicating with their dormitories, which were above the inmates' day rooms.

The 'superior officers' (the charge nurses of the day) had their own apartments, so arranged to enable them to supervise the whole of the department over which they had charge.

In 1861 the main entrance was fronted by huge wrought iron gates and flanked by two square buildings. The building on the left of the gate contained the Porter's residence, clothing store and probationary ward. This was a sort of admission ward where prospective inmates could change their own clothing for 'comfortable' (and more often than not, cleaner) Union clothing. (In 1927 part of this building was the Engineer's residence and became my home - our address was 'Old Lodge'.) The building is still standing and is at present staff accommodation. The building on the right of the gateway, now demolished, contained the Boardroom for committee meetings of the Board of Guardians and waiting rooms for the interviewing of staff and other purposes. (In later years the building was transformed into a nurses' home and was known affectionately by the staff as 'Hollywood'.)

Beyond these two buildings, up a landscaped garden and path and under the tower was the main building. Through an imposing entrance were the apartments, or quarters, as they were known, of the Master and Matron. Also in the main building were Male and Female wards, kitchen and dining room and a block for the Female Sick.

To the west of the main building was the cemetery, which was in use until about 1934. The site is approximately opposite the recently-built H and J Wards. The roadway was made 10 feet wide to the entrance and a chapel was built inside the grounds. The different areas of 'class' were divided by gravel walkways. The cemetery was planned to contain 1,000 graves: 556 CofE and 444 Nonconformists - no mention of Roman Catholics.

The Male side of the main building, later Carr Ward and now L4, housed the day rooms and bedrooms for the men and a day room and seven bedrooms for aged married couples; two bedrooms for infants and their mothers, and two rooms for 'lying-in' women.

The Female ward was similarly arranged for elderly women; there were also linen and needlework rooms and rooms for Juniors and Girls. One room housed a monster cradle to rock

8

half a dozen babies to sleep at one time. There was a wash-house on the female side to the rear of the day rooms.

Next to the dormitories for women and girls were rooms of wooden washing troughs. Every trough had taps of hot and cold water - quite a luxury in those early days. There was room for 30 women and 26 girls and there were enough troughs for them all to wash at the same time. The floors sloped towards the centre and a deep stone channel carried away waste water.

The water for the wash boilers was heated by steam - it was considered cleaner and more economical than open furnaces. In the drying and ironing rooms, the fronts of the drying stoves had iron frames to which were fixed wooden clothes horses. These drew out on iron rails, let flush into the floor.

Incorporated on the Male side was the tailor's shop, where suits were made and altered, and a shoemaker's and shoe repair department. For able-bodied men there were buildings in the yard where various tasks were carried on, such as corn-grinding and oakum-picking. (The latter involved un-picking old ropes so that the pieces could be re-used in waterproofing boats.) At the rear of the yard for boys and girls were plunge baths - one way of keeping clean.

The Dining Room was majestic. It was 75 feet long, 66 feet wide and 27 feet high. There was a raised platform at one end, from

*Master and Matron's living quarters and Male Infirm to the right. The premises are now offices and L4 respectively. (Photographed in 1962)*

which the Governor could overlook the inmates at mealtimes and also conduct Services. There were cast iron gratings in the floor for hot-air heating. The windows were large and long, making the huge room light and airy. A balcony was added along the back wall at a later date. The 600 inmates could be accommodated all at the same time on 96 tables.

To the rear of the dining room, outside, was a two-stalled stable, with hayroom and cart shed. Above the cart shed was a bedroom, where the stoker slept. Also attached to the back of the Dining Room were the Bakehouse and the Boilerhouse; these premises are still there, but used for other purposes. The Bakehouse was put to other uses when the bread, ready baked and sliced, was delivered, and the Boilerhouse is now part of the laundry — the clean sorting area and linen room.

From the Boilerhouse stone steps led to the ten cellars, where milk, larder supplies and general stores were kept. They were ventilated by iron gratings. The gas pipes and water mains were also in these cellars — thus facilitating re-laying or repair of any pipes without injuring the floor or interfering with the regular routine of the House.

The main windows of the Workhouse were large and double hung, allowing plenty of light and good ventilation. The size of the windows also permitted full, undetected inspection of day rooms and Dining Room by the Master and other senior staff.

Cast iron gratings in the floor of the upper corridors gave light through to the corridors on the ground floor and also provided a means of ventilation. During the construction of the main building, inlet air flues were formed in the piers of the side walls, next to the corridors, with outlet flues for the escape of vitiated air near the ceiling line. All inlet and outlet flues were fitted with regulation air grids, and a large number of extracting ventilators (manufactured by Howorth's of Farnworth) were fixed on the ridges of the various roofs. Each day room was fitted with 'dust shoots' — small doors fixed near the floor line through which ashes from the fireplaces were discharged to the basement. There was an upright water pipe on the landing of each staircase. The pipes had brass union joints, to which gutta-percha hoses could be fixed instantly in case of fire.

All these up-to-date fittings and conveniences must have seemed wonderful to the care and maintenance staff; whether they were appreciated by the inmates is another question! However, the provision of hot water, light and heat meant far better care and cleanliness than the poor people had had in their basic cottages.

## The Early Years

On 28th September 1861 the members of the Board of Guardians, together with other influential people of Bolton, processed through the building to the Dining Room for the opening ceremony, which began with the hymn 'Praise to the Lord, 'tis good to raise'. In the evening a celebratory dinner was held for the Board of Guardians; Mr R Holt of the Church Hotel, Kearsley, did the catering.

In July 1864 there were 558 inmates in the main Workhouse. In addition, there were 101 Lunatics, 3 suffering from smallpox, 8 suffering from 'itch' (presumably skin rashes caused by vermin, scabies, etc) and 24 vagrants. In that month there were 36 admissions, 23 discharges, 3 deaths and no births.

More buildings were being added in 1864; by August a new female wing was almost finished. Two new blocks for the infirm (now Russell wards) were built later. One block was demolished in the late 1930s and stood next to Russell Vickers Ward, on the site of the present maintenance workshops.

On 12th October 1864 the Board of Guardians were invited to the opening of Farnworth Park and the children of the Workhouse were to be included in the civic procession. Around this time the Workhouse Committee, made up of members of the Board of Guardians, was formed. The Committee visited the Workhouse periodically and supervised the running of the institution.

In November 1864 a female 'lunatic' attendant applied for a rise of £4 per year – her salary was about £20 per year. This was refused at the Committee meeting. At their December meeting the Workhouse Committee discussed the practice of putting Workhouse girls out to work at public houses in the surrounding districts. It was said that such girls could be wrongly influenced. However, in defence of the working girls, one member stated that a girl working in a Little Hulton public house was cleaner, very tidy and respectable and was attending Sunday School. Members in favour of girls working outside said that the Guardians were not justified in keeping these children at the expense of the ratepayers when they could be well cared for and respectably brought up.

It was around this time that the Guardians discussed whether the inmates were warm enough. The majority said not, so more coal was ordered for all fires. This was cheaper than moving the hot water pipes from the cellars to the corridors, where they would have been 'unsightly' anyway.

The Master was questioned about the amount and quality of food for children of two years and over. Mr Greenhalgh agreed to the menu suggested by the Workhouse Committee, which was as follows:

Breakfast & Supper every day: 3oz bread, $\frac{1}{2}$ pint milk porridge

Dinners: Monday 3 oz bread      Tuesday 3 oz bread
              2 oz beef                      $\frac{1}{4}$ oz butter
              $\frac{1}{4}$ lb potatoes               $\frac{1}{2}$ pint coffee
              $\frac{1}{2}$ pint broth

Wednesday 3 oz bread
½ pint rice milk
(probably rice pudding)

Thursday 3 oz bread
2 oz beef
¼ lb potatoes
½ pint broth

Friday 3 oz bread
1 oz cheese
½ pint coffee

Saturday 3 oz bread
½ pint pea soup

Sunday 3 oz bread
1 oz cheese
½ pint coffee

Whilst not a very varied or interesting diet, it appears to contain all the necessary nutrients. The consumption of large amounts of coffee would not have been helpful for children, however.

Between 1868 and 1871 tramps and paupers were becoming a problem. In 1869 a long report was published concerning the treatment of tramps. It was said that in the common lodging houses in the town three married couples slept rough in one room, whilst in the Tramp Ward at the Workhouse men and women were properly separated. In spite of this, the young men and women seemed to enjoy the vagrant life; they had no responsibilities, the open countryside to wander in and a bed and meal for the night, provided they behaved themselves. It was estimated that there were between 70,000 and 80,000 tramps wandering the country.

At the Workhouse they had to be in the Tramp Ward by 9.00pm. Late comers had to report to the Police, and they were probably put in a cell for the night. In 1869 the number of vagrants, paupers and sick people was increasing; sometimes as many as seven people were taken in in one day. There were 116 more inmates than the previous year, 50 more vagrants and 10 un-employed able-bodied men.

Because of the increase in the number of pregnant inmates, a Nurse/Midwife was appointed in 1869. She transferred from Liverpool Workhouse and was paid £20 per year, plus food and uniform.

In 1870 it was discovered that one of the 'paupers' who had received relief money to help him live at home had left £9 to each of his children in his Will. Others were found to have money hidden away. They were obviously after all they could get!

In 1871 there was much discussion at the Guardians' meetings about tramps arriving in Bolton. Where could they be housed other than in Fishpool? Nothing was done, and in July 1872 the problem had not gone away. During the first six months of that year, 5,000 tramps had arrived in the town, hoping for a night's accommodation. A further 4,500 arrived at the Workhouse alone during the second half of the year.

12

The Guardians considered the siting of a new Tramp Ward. Should they use part of the Workhouse, or build one in the town? A tramp ward for women and children in town was suggested, in order to save them trailing to Fishpool in bad weather.

In 1871 a woman of 'unsound mind' was admitted from Darcy Lever. Her savings of £18 were put towards her maintenance. An inmate suffering from delirium tremens was put in a padded cell on the lunatic ward. He was so violent that he damaged the cell, and was made to pay for the necessary repairs.

The case of a monomaniac, who had been committed to Prestwich lunatic asylum by the Borough Magistrate, was raised. The asylum wanted the patient to be referred to Fishpool Workhouse. The Master considered that the man would not be a danger to other inmates and that he would fit in well. There was at this time an 'exchange' of acutely insane and chronic inmates between Prestwich and Fishpool. If Prestwich was full, and had no chronically insane inmates to exchange, then Chester asylum was used.

Around the same time Mr Greenhalgh, the Master, was called to see a man at Harrison's Bakehouse in Horwich, following a 'fall'. The man was found to be an epileptic and not a lunatic. Because he was homeless as well, the man was taken to the Workhouse to be cared for.

At a Committee meeting on 22nd November 1871 it was disclosed that Australian corned mutton had been tried out. This was found to be more economical than English beef, being boxed already cooked and with no bones. All agreed that it tasted very nice.

In 1872 a new Fever Hospital was completed and is still standing, next to the present Day Hospital. 'Fever Hospital 1872' is inscribed in the stonework at the top of the building, between the towers. Inmates with varying conditions of infection were taken into the new block. Illnesses from typhus to 'the itch' and odd cases of smallpox were treated. In August 1873 cases of smallpox occurred and part of the new Fever Hospital was partitioned off to isolate the infected patients. Today the building houses the Departments of Clinical Psychology and Medical Illustration.

The returns for December 1872 were:
Inmates 450    Admissions 37    Births 2    Vagrants helped 170
Children 24    Discharges 17    Deaths 6

In August 1873 the Workhouse Committee discussed whether to board out six children to respectable families, instead of keeping them in the Workhouse. Against boarding out, it was said that the children had received the best of attention from the

Master, Matron and staff. The children had been brought into the Workhouse from the streets and, to quote one member of the Committee, 'They were the swillings of the gutter and the savages of civilisation'. After being cleaned up, decently fed and treated properly, they were fit to receive some kind of education from the school, and since they had been at the Workhouse they were so physically and morally changed that they would not have been recognised as the same beings. If they were put out to families, one member said, there would always be the risk of physical abuse. It was decided by 14 votes to 13 that the experiment of boarding out should be tried.

Whilst living in the Workhouse, children seemed to be encouraged to take part in outside activities, such as the Whit Walks. On 27th August 1873 Roman Catholic children were allowed to attend the laying of the foundation stone of St Gregory's Chapel in Farnworth.

## Local Government Board Inspections

Once a year there was an inspection of the Workhouse by two representatives from the Local Government Board of Whitehall, London. On one visit the inspectors noted that in the lunatic wards 12 men and 8 women had died in less than nine months. They observed that this high mortality pointed to the fact that the amount of animal food (presumably meat products) given to this class was insufficient and should, therefore, be increased. Two other deaths occurred at this time; a man was found dead from epilepsy and a woman, who got through a window, was found drowned in a pond a short distance away. The Inspectors' Report also contained an item about a man suffering from 'general paralysis' (perhaps a stroke, or, as he was in the lunatic ward, general paralysis of the insane) and stated that he should be kept under observation by the Medical Officer, as he was likely to get worse and be 'unfit for treatment in the Workhouse.' Presumably this meant that the man needed proper hospital care and nursing which could not be given in the lunatic ward.

On discovering that the inmates had cotton bed gowns all year round, the inspectors recommended that in future night wear should be made of linsey (a coarse material of inferior wool woven on cotton warp). Whether this advice was given for reasons of economy or warmth is not stated.

Twelve to eighteen men worked on the land, and few other inmates were employed. Mat making was suggested by the inspectors, as it was considered a safe but useful occupation. They thought that knitting should be introduced for the women inmates who had nothing to do. Ten to fourteen were already employed in sewing and repairing inmates' clothing. Other women did a considerable amount of cleaning, washing and assisting generally in the running of the Workhouse. Between

14

twenty-five and thirty of either sex attended chapel regularly. These figures suggest that at this time (1873) Church attendance was not compulsory. All who were able were sent for walks round the grounds at the back of the Workhouse. The inspectors recommended that a double row of trees be planted to make an avenue, and that seats be provided for the inmates to have a rest during their exercise.

The inspectors also suggested that:
1. Knives, forks and tablecloths should be supplied in the various day rooms.
2. Flock or horsehair should be used instead of straw for the beds of patients and inmates of clean habits. Under-blankets should be placed upon all straw mattresses, and the sides of cots or beds used by epileptics should be padded.
3. All women should be provided with single beds.
4. Bells, communicating with the attendants' room, should be placed in each dormitory so that help could be summoned.
5. Leather shoes should be provided for indoor use, instead of cheap slippers.
6. Lavatories on upper floors should be brought into use. (Presumably these had been neglected and unused.) Combs and brushes should also be supplied.
7. A paid night nurse, who could also give some assistance during the day, should be appointed to each department. (When these nurses were expected to sleep is not stated!)

The Tramp Ward had been built to accommodate 16, and it was becoming very overcrowded - 23 sharing 16 cells was typical. The Guardians argued that 30 cells would have been a more realistic number to build from the start. The building of a tramp ward in the town was again discussed, this time for 16 males and 8 females.

Tramps were a continual problem. In order to find out more about them, the Master of the Workhouse decided to keep a record of their visits, noting age, medical history and other particulars. If it was found that the 'professional' tramps visited too frequently, the tramp superintendent would find these men harder tasks, such as breaking large stones. The superintendent also tried to help the tramps towards living properly - the 1873 version of attempts at rehabilitation. If there was no room at Fishpool, or if the tramps were unsuitable, tickets were issued so that they could go to common lodging houses in Bolton.

In 1873 the children of the Institution took part in the Bolton Whit Walks. Whilst walking in Churchgate they were given oranges, buns and ginger beer by Mr Weston, and buns and coffee by Mr Flitcroft (both prominent local businessmen), when the procession passed their houses. In the November of that year Mary Jones (aged 9), John Buckley (13) and George Berry (14) were sent to work for local businessmen.

In 1875 periodic leave of absence for inmates was granted. Not more than 20 were allowed out at one time; male and female had to go out on separate days, and only from 9.00am to 6.00pm. If misbehaviour was reported or rules were broken, the leave was stopped.

The Guardians suggested that a library be set up for the inmates. One member, Mr Ormerod, started the library with the donation of a few books.

In 1876, after someone had been attacked by a lunatic, it was decided to change the uniform clothing. Two different sets were now to be worn, to distinguish the lunatics from the general inmates.

At a Workhouse Committee meeting, Mr Ormerod asked if anything was being done to lessen the consumption of spirits and beer in the Workhouse. He reported that Wrexham Workhouse had abolished spirits with some success. One member argued that spirits were being given by the Workhouse Doctor, and it was for him to decide what spirits and beer should be given out. In 1875 the cost of intoxicants, borne by the Guardians, was as follows: Wine £3/15/10d; Gin £24/2/1d; Brandy £15/14/11d; Beer £100/2/2d. The total of £143/15/- was higher than in previous years, but in defence of the figures, the Doctor said that alcohol, and gin in particular, was a very good medicine. In the debate that followed, Wrexham was quoted as having 89 inmates who had survived over 60 years, with an average age of 73 years (a very good age in those days). The oldest inmate there was 96 and had been in the regular habit of having a drop of spirits until three years previously. Since then, without alcoholic stimulants, he and the other inmates had led a healthy and comfortable life. 'If Wrexham could do that, Fishpool could do it.' A vote was taken and it was resolved that the supply of alcohol should be discontinued.

In 1879 older children (3 to 16 years) ceased to be little inmates at Fishpool and became residents of cottage homes adjacent to the Workhouse. There were originally four cottages and a school; two more cottages were built in 1880 and when the scheme was eventually completed there were ten cottages and two school buildings. The buildings formed a square, with grass in the middle, and swings and parallel horizontal bars were placed on the grass for recreation.

Each cottage accommodated 30 children. On the ground floor were a large day room, dining room, kitchen and scullery, and lavatory. Upstairs were three dormitories and a bedroom for the house-parents. Girls were given domestic training in preparation for going into service and the boys were given industrial training to enable them to earn a living, and become useful members of society.

Transferring the children from the Workhouse removed them from
16

the 'evil influences' of paupers and tramps, and made room available in the Workhouse for more paupers as the town's population increased.

In 1884 the original cookhouse and breadroom was made into a Chapel for Holy Communion; this was used by Roman Catholics as well as Church of England and Free Church members.

There was concern for the physical safety of the inmates as well as for their spiritual welfare. The same year, direct communication with the Fire Station was inaugurated, so that the arrival of the Fire Brigade would be much quicker if there was a fire.

In 1885 Mr and Mrs Ratheram had succeeded Mr and Mrs Pilling (themselves successors to Mr and Mrs Greenhalgh) as Master and Matron. In the June of that year Mrs Ratheram appointed a new nurse (at £20 per annum), who came from Chorlton-on-Medlock Institution in Manchester. She replaced a Mrs Williamson, who had become a patient at Fishpool.

In June 1885 a little boy was found at Trinity Street Station and placed in the Workhouse. The finder, who lived in Harwood, applied to adopt the child, as did many other people when the story appeared in the local paper. At the July meeting of the Board of Guardians, the Medical Officer reported that the child might be suffering from an hereditary disease and so the decision regarding adoption was postponed. Later, the Master, Mr Ratherham, allowed the child to go to the Harwood people. Then someone in Horwich offered the couple £5 for the child. For the sake of the little boy, and to save a lot of trouble, the Harwood couple gave up their claim in favour of the Horwich couple. All that the Guardians were concerned about was that the child should have a comfortable home.

Capable inmates who were reliable and honest were given jobs in administration, whilst the less clever were given manual jobs around the houses and grounds - gardening, looking after the pigs, boilers and so on. John Entwistle was given a job in the Master's office at 5/- per week. This was a great chance for him, as an inmate employed in this capacity could work his way up and become a senior clerk, or even Master of an institution.

On the weekend of 23 July 1885 the figures were:
    Inmates 683 (624 in 1884)
    Admissions 40    Births 2    Discharged 28    Deaths 6
    Imbeciles/Idiots 28    Erysipelas 5    Scarlatina 1    Rubella 1
    Scabies 1

By August the number of inmates had increased to 738. It was ordered that additional baths be built.

In that year the Local Government Board instituted a grant of $£20\frac{1}{2}$ per annum for John Pilling and Joseph Taylor, teachers in shoemaking and tailoring. There were no grants available for

17

teachers with classes of less than six boys, and teachers appeared to be in a sort of competency league. For example, certificates awarded to the Schoolmaster and Mistress, Mr Tomlinson and Miss Ormerod, were marked 'Efficient – first division', and they were given annual grants of £60 and £48 respectively. Miss Whiteside, Assistant Mistress, was given a certificate marked 'Competency 2nd division' and a grant of £20. All monies came from the Local Government Board, and not Bolton's ratepayers.

At that time 60 Workhouse children were working in service in the town. They had regular visits from Relieving Officers (forerunners of Social Workers), who reported that the children were living in satisfactory conditions.

After a visit in September 1885 the Government Inspector reported that the diet for persons of unsound mind was grossly inadequate and many of them were suffering from physical disorders as well. He noted that there was not a single solid fresh meat dish in the week, the hash being made like soup, and there seemed to be a disregard for bathing; some imbeciles had not been bathed for several years. As there were only 13 males and 17 females of unsound mind, he thought this was disgraceful. The imbeciles were subsequently bathed fortnightly. (The liquid diet was probably to lessen the risk of them choking on their food.)

The bedding was now judged to be fairly good, although some sheets were found to be ragged and worn out. Personal clothing was said to be poor and untidy; the inspector recommended that the staff should encourage the patients to look smarter.

In April 1886 the following contracts were awarded to local firms:
Flax sheeting and women's corsets: Stubbs Bros, Deansgate
Grey winceyette blankets and mob caps for women: Quinney & Co, Derby Street
Calico (for sheeting): James Dean, Halliwell Road
Blue flannel: C Callis, Bradshawgate
Scouring flannel: Best & Eyland, Oxford Street
Candlewick warp and weft (for weaving): Barlow & Jones Ltd, Albert and Prospect Mills

Later in the year the children were invited by Mr Elliston, manager of the Theatre Royal, to his pantomime. Mr Tom Hamer of the Queen Elizabeth Hotel, and friends, gave sweets and oranges for them to eat during the show. Mr Hamer and friends also gave concerts at the Workhouse for the inmates. For all these extra Christmas festivities, these kind people received the thanks of the Board of Guardians.

In 1887 boys were sent from the Workhouse to join the Merchant Navy. This was a good chance for them to prove themselves; having learned discipline in the Workhouse they would work hard on the ships.

Some improvements were suggested at this time. It was decided to add gates at the back of the Fever Block. The gates, low wall and railings which surrounded the building were built well out, enclosing a considerable area of land, presumably to isolate the block. In the 1930s the first tennis court was opened in the grounds on this land; the present Day Hospital now stands on the site. In November 1887 Mr J Brearley of Farnworth, a member of the Workhouse Committee, suggested that a clock be placed in the tower, but this idea never came to fruition. The same month, the first paid cook was appointed, the previous ones having been inmates. It was a joint appointment; the cook was paid £20 per year and her husband, as storekeeper, was paid £40, with food and accommodation provided.

## Allegations of Scandal

In November 1889 one Mary Cabanis accused two other inmates of stealing a package containing six sovereigns from a ledge outside a dormitory window. Mrs Cabanis became quite violent and had to be restrained in a strait jacket. An attendant subsequently found 54 sovereigns under Mrs Cabanis' pillow. It transpired that she was in the habit of concealing little parcels of money about her person and she was found to be deluded about people stealing her money. The lady became so violent that she was transferred to Prestwich Asylum.

Mary Cabanis (nee Smith) had come to Bolton with her two sisters from Cumberland. The sisters went to live in Gas Street and Mary became a housekeeper to a Salford businessman, looking after his country residence and attending to guests at his shooting lodge at Entwistle. When she was sixty years old the gentleman placed her in a residence in Deane Lane, Daubhill, presumably to enjoy her retirement. However, Mary started to drink and became confused, and this was when the money that she had carefully saved from her wages was wrapped up in packets and hidden between layers of her clothes. It was because of her abnormal behaviour that she was placed in Fishpool Workhouse. When she was transferred to Prestwich after the alleged theft her sisters protested strongly, saying that she was not mentally ill. But it was to no avail, and Mary spent the rest of her life in the asylum.

At the time of the Mary Cabanis incident, there was a scandal at the Workhouse which received wide publicity in Bolton and beyond. Dr Marsh, the Medical Officer, had in his possession letters allegedly sent by some prominent members of the Board of Guardians, including the Mayor, to Rose Morris, a nurse at the Workhouse, suggesting immoral relations between the nurse and certain members of the Board. Dr Marsh believed the letters to be genuine, and made grave accusations against the members. For this he was suspended from duty, along with Rose Morris. However, Board members were so strong in their denials that Dr Marsh apologised and offered to produce the letters, now believing that they were forgeries. The Guardians voted to reject the doctor's apology and decided that there must be an inquiry.

The Bolton Chronicle commented: '...*it was the Guardians' solemn duty to leave no stone unturned to have the matter probed to the bottom. The immorality which had been accumulating under their auspices for years requires cleaning out, not covering over...Some of our public men are either unfit for the high positions they hold, or characters are being wantonly aspersed...*'

The Local Government Inspector came to Bolton on Wednesday December 11th 1889 and the Inquiry was fixed for the 20th December. Unfortunately, Rose Morris had died of 'syncope' (heart blockage) and aneurism, brought about by the stress of the scandal, on 23rd November. In addition, Dr Morris and the implicated Guardians had destroyed the letters, making it impossible to prove or disprove the allegations. Some Workhouse servants gave evidence, saying that they had seen certain Guardians visiting Rose Morris at unusual hours, but the inquiry chose not to believe their statements. On 15th March 1890 the Local Government Board decided that there had been no misconduct by any Guardian and exonerated them from all charges. Dr Morris had resigned in February 1890.

# Taking on Staff

Recruiting nurses to care for the sick and lunatic inmates seemed to present difficulties. The Board of Guardians paid a £5 annual subscription to the Northern Workhouses Nurses' Association for a supply of trained nurses (or the equivalent of that day). One such nurse, living in Waterloo Street, Crumpsall, left her job after just 24 hours because she could not manage the lunatics and epileptics. As a result of this, and one or two other failures with the Nurses' Association, the Board decided to make their own appointments using local nurses.

Continued improvement in overall care included a celebration dinner for inmates on the occasion of the Royal Wedding on 6th July 1893 (the future King George V and Queen Mary). The dinner included roast beef and plum pudding, and the children were each given an orange and a bag of sweets.

In 1893 the Rev H W Turner, a member of the Nonconformist Ministers' Association, appealed to the Board of Guardians to give the same consideration to the Nonconformist inmates as they gave to Church of England and Roman Catholic adherents. As a result, in later years, Nonconformist Services took place on a Sunday afternoon, following the Roman Catholic and Church of England services in the morning. Early in 1893, the Salford Diocese asked the Guardians if there were any Roman Catholic children, aged eight and upwards, for consideration for emigration to Canada. It was reported that no suitable children were found. Whether any child went at a later date is not recorded. It seems incredible now that children so young should be sent so far away.

In May 1893 the Board decided that a suitable site should be found on which to build a new isolation block so that infected inmates would not be in the wards with other inmates. By June plans had been made for this block to contain 20 beds for infected patients, excluding those with smallpox and typhus. Patients suffering from these diseases were moved to Rumworth Hospital (probably Hulton Lane) at a cost to the Guardians of £5 per week. (As it happened, there was an outbreak of small-pox in 1893.)

The new isolation block, a long, single storey building, cost £1,500 to build. The architects were Woodhouse & Potts of Bolton and the builder was Samuel Hodgkiss of Farnworth. This isolation block was probably intended for inmates suffering from tuberculosis, as there was a verandah on the south side (for fresh air) and a concrete patio running the length of the building, on to which the beds could be pulled.

When it ceased to be a fever hospital, one half of the building was occupied by the cook, Mr Scholes, and his wife, who was the laundress. They were both appointed in 1905, as assistant cook and assistant laundress, at salaries of £40 and £20 per annum. About 1936 we (the Engineer's family) moved to the other half of the building from the Old Porter's Lodge, which was too small. In 1956 the block was altered and extended and became the School of Nursing. Today it houses the Bolton College of Nursing, with further extensions and alterations having been made.

A detached house for the resident Medical Officers was built adjacent to the new infectious diseases hospital. There were living quarters for domestic staff at the top of the house. In later years this house became the residence of Mr Farrell and his family. Mr Farrell was the Townleys Hospital Steward (fore-runner of the Hospital Secretary), and after he retired in 1939, the house became known as the Engineer's House, my family's third and last residence in the grounds. At present the house stands empty.

In 1894 gradual improvements were noticeable in the Workhouse. Tobacco and snuff allowances were being considered for certain inmates — probably those who worked in the buildings and grounds. Lady Visitors, who began to be much in evidence at this time, recommended a 'hot and cold lavatory' for the 'lying-in' wards. (This possibly meant a low wash basin with hot and cold running water.) The Ladies also recommended that metal 'mess tins', used in the infirm wards, should be replaced by pint pots and this was done.

In May 1894 it was decided to advertise for a laundress to

supervise the washing and ironing of inmates' clothes, at a salary of £25 per year, plus food and apartments. June saw an effort to improve the care of the sick inmates, when a lady superintendent and additional nursing staff were appointed. Indeed, the Resident Medical Officer commented that the Workhouse was becoming more of a sick hospital than an institution for the able poor.

More children were being taken into the Workhouse. Three Roman Catholic boys were sent to an industrial training residence at Buckley Hall, Rochdale, and ten girls to Hollymount boarding school at Tottington. Four other children were to be boarded out under the auspices of the Ladies' Boarding-out Committee; they had boarded out as many as 20 in previous weeks.

Bovril was tried out as an alternative beverage for the inmates.

There was still difficulty in recruiting staff and so in 1894 some nurses were again supplied by the Northern Workhouses Nurses' Association. These nurses were again found to be unsatisfactory.

The new tramp ward in Bolton (Kingsgate) was still not completed, so it was decided to open an extra ward at the Workhouse to make room for the increasing number of tramps. Mr Blower was the Superintendent of the tramp ward at Fishpool. (He may have been a relative of Miss Blower, a Superintendent nurse in the 1930s and a respected lady in Farnworth.)

Kingsgate was finally opened in Idle Lane, Bolton, in 1898, to cater for tramps arriving in the town. So they no longer had to be taken two or three miles to Fishpool.

In 1894 the Workhouse Committee was adamant that a separate lunatic ward was neither desirable nor necessary at Fishpool. The reasoning behind this decision is not known. It may have been to the advantage of the mentally ill for them to mix with well people, whatever the risk to those more normal inmates. However, this ruling was not permanent, as I recall that from the 1930s until further improvements and freedom in later years, mentally ill elderly were locked away in the block now known as Russell Vickers. Iron bars covered the windows and side doors (no longer there) had iron bars across the openings so that the solid doors could be left open in the summer. The main doors at the front were always kept locked. This block also contained the padded rooms for obstreperous patients, one on the male side and one on the female side.

On 4th October 1894 it was decided to purchase adjoining land from the Townleys estate so that the institution could be extended. £10,000 was borrowed to buy 76 acres. Two blocks were later built on the new site and these were used to accommodate sick people who needed nursing, keeping them separate from the Workhouse, which was already overcrowded with poor and destitute inmates. The old fever hospital, built in

1872, had already been extended to accommodate more sick cases – 87 male and 87 female.

Appointments made this year included a Medical Officer, Dr John Morris, at a salary of £70 per year, and a laundress at £27 plus rations and apartments. The latter, who came from Clyde Street, Cheetham Hill, Manchester, received £2 'beer money' – an incentive, perhaps?

Alteration and improvement of inmates' clothing was being considered in 1894. The Board of Guardians instructed the Workhouse Committee to order 100 suits of 'ordinary' cloth for the paupers who were inmates through no fault of their own, and whose conduct as inmates rendered them deserving of being clothed in a different manner from the 'worthless, destitute and lazy', whose rough uniform was well known as a badge of degradation. This idea had been tried some ten years earlier, but it was found that some of the inmates, on getting good clothes, went outside and pawned them! The Workhouse Committee decided to try kitting out a few inmates at a time as an experiment. It was noted that the idea had been tried at Islington Workhouse in London, and had been successful.

The subject of alcohol was raised again in 1898. The general use of alcohol had been banned some years earlier and it was only available when prescribed by the Medical Officer. One exception to the rule was the special allowance with Christmas Dinner, and some members of the Workhouse Committee thought that this should be discontinued. Others said that because a man was down in the world, why deprive him of his glass of beer at Christmas? Those in favour of the ban remarked that beer whetted the appetite for more to drink – the curse that had brought some of them into the Workhouse in the first place.

Apparently there had been 'disgraceful scenes of drunkenness' after the Christmas Dinner the year before. One member commented that the 'disgraceful scenes' were grossly exaggerated, and that some of the Guardians were never happy unless they were making people miserable! After the debate, the vote was 20 for the provision of beer and 24 against. So for Christmas 1898 the inmates had to make do with tea or coffee.

Following the decision to put new buildings on Townleys land, a new Nurses' Home was suggested. This was completed in 1901, and is still used for accommodation for nurses.

# Taking Stock; Entertainments

At the beginning of 1901 there were 1,057 inmates, an increase of 114 on the corresponding period in 1900. There were 70 in the Tramp Ward, 5 infectious cases (all scabies), 494 sick in the hospital block and 693 lunatics.

A new Master and Matron, Mr and Mrs Booth, were appointed in 1901, succeeding Mr and Mrs Davies, who had retired.

In the December the Chairman of the Workhouse Committee, Mr Cunliffe, proposed the usual Christmas Dinner for inmates on 26th December. This was to include a limited amount of roast beef and plum pudding, with one pint of tea, coffee, cocoa or milk for each inmate. There would be snuff and tobacco for adults and oranges and nuts for children. Boxing Day was the inmates' day for celebration at Christmas time until about 1963. This was so that the Mayor, Councillors and Board of Guardians could have their Christmas Day at home with their families and visit the Workhouse on Boxing day, meeting staff and inmates.

The treatment of sane epileptics was being considered by other Unions in the North. Blackburn Union had sent a circular to the Bolton and other Boards, stating that they were 'desirous of founding a colony of separate homes for the suitable care and treatment of sane epileptics, in a purpose-built institution'. They had appointed a committee to formulate a scheme and invited representatives from other Unions to a conference on the matter in Blackburn. The Blackburn Board of Guardians believed that it was better for young epileptics to be cared for separately, and not in lunatic asylums. The Bolton Workhouse Committee Chairman said that 'Epileptics at Fishpool were adequately looked after, being trained for suitable work, and in spite of an increase in epilepsy in young people at that time, were being housed separately at the Workhouse'.

A good example of this within memory was a young man called Jimmy, a severe epileptic and inmate at Fishpool during the 1930s and 1940s. He was trained to be an upholsterer whilst in the Workhouse, and he covered chairs and stools made to last. He made one for my father, which I still possess. Jimmy also did any odd job or errand that needed doing, having many a severe fit in the process. There were no drugs to control epilepsy in those days, except perhaps phenobarbitone, which was not as effective as present-day medication.

With the completion of the new Nurses' Home in 1901, it was time to think about the training of nurses for promotion to charge nurses, instead of appointing staff from outside. However, as there was not yet a scheme for this, the Guardians appointed a Miss Hopkins from Scarborough as charge nurse, with a salary of £40 per year and her keep. Nurses were to have their own Medical Officer, and Dr Laslett of Farnworth was appointed to this duty at a fee of 10/6d per nurse.

The same year, the Workhouse organist, Mr Abraham Wood, was required to play the organ for the Church of England service every Sunday afternoon, as well as for the Nonconformist service in the evening. In May, because of this extra work, his allowance was increased from £5 to £10 per year.

The school was no longer situated in the first two cottages and children were now attending outside schools. Because of this, parents could visit their children in the Cottage Homes only on the first and third Saturday monthly, though special permission to visit at other times could be obtained.

Mrs Greg, a benevolent lady who was a member of the Board of Guardians, gave £40 for two summer houses for inmates suffering from tuberculosis. These were placed on the lawns in front of the main block, and one was still there until recent years.

The Board of Guardians' subscription to the Bolton Royal Infirmary in 1901 was 50 guineas, which entitled the Union to have treatment for 25 in-patients and 100 outdoor casualties or out-patients. All these were poor persons receiving outdoor relief, although they were encouraged to go to the Workhouse whenever possible, rather than to the Infirmary. 50 guineas were also subscribed to Bolton District Nurses' Association, for the treatment of sick in their own homes, and ten guineas went to the Farnworth District Nurses' Association. The Royal Eye Hospital in Manchester received a subscription of 10 guineas for the treatment of 25 out-patients and 10 in-patients.

Meanwhile, staffing of the Nurses' Home was being arranged. Instead of using pauper help, the Committee engaged three servants at £18 each per year. Parts of the new general hospital, which were being built by this time, were also being run without pauper help. This, of course, was a progressive step.

1902 was Coronation Year and children and adults alike had special treats on Saturday 26th June. They also took part in the town's festivities on the Thursday and Friday of the following week. Bunting and flags were festooned everywhere in the grounds and inside the various buildings. Sports events for the children and younger inmates took place in the grounds, whilst the older ones looked on. Beef, ham, currant cake and tobacco were provided. Sick inmates and those unable to go out in the grounds for other reasons were provided with special entertainment inside. The cost of all this came directly out of the rates and not from the Workhouse funds set aside for the children's annual seaside outing – they would still have that later. There was also double outdoor relief in Coronation Week for the poor outside the Workhouse.

Earlier in the year, the Board of Guardians agreed to give 3/- each to the Roman Catholic children boarded out at Hollymount Home, Tottington, towards their seaside outing. For others boarded out at private homes, it was 1/- only, presumably because the other homes had more resources than Hollymount, which relied on voluntary contributions. In August 1902 the children were removed from Hollymount because of unsatisfactory conditions. However, the home was reopened in late September under new administration, and a new 'Certificate of Satisfaction' had been given. A letter from the Sisters of Charity, now running the school, was sent to the Board of Guardians inviting inspection, but the Guardians would not let the children return.

In 1902 the Master of the Workhouse decided that the names of vagrants who were convicted criminals should be posted up in the Tramp Ward as a warning to other, possibly criminal, vagrants.

In September 1902 a Workhouse boy had five strokes of the birch for twice running away to Manchester. One member of the Guardians, James Tonge, strongly objected, saying that birching had a degrading and demoralising effect upon children. Councillor Webster replied, 'that if Mr Tonge had as much knowledge of boys' behaviour, as he and other members had, he would not object or condemn birching'.

In December 1902 two women inmates, Elizabeth McNulty and Sara Laithwaite, were confined in separate rooms on a diet of bread and water for 24 hours for being 'cheeky' to staff and generally insubordinate.

It was at this time that the Bolton Guardians severely restricted indiscriminate relief, especially to professional beggars, on vagrant wards. This had the effect of making more room available for genuine vagrants in trouble. The public were also cautioned against giving to professional beggars, as it was an encouragement to avoid work. There was also a complaint that there was a great deal of immorality amongst single women, who in consequence had to go to the Workhouse, causing much expense to the ratepayers.

At the end of the year, birching was still being carried out, despite the protests made earlier. Four boys had six strokes each for misbehaviour, in front of the other boys as a warning to them.

Boxing Day in 1902 was a Friday and a Roman Catholic member of the Guardians asked if the Christmas Dinner could be moved to the Saturday, or if the RC inmates could have fish instead of beef. The Guardians agreed to have the Christmas Dinner on the Saturday that year.

By July 1903 five lady members were installed on the Board of Guardians, which was quite an innovation for those days. As a result, the Ladies' Visiting Committee became unnecessary and was later disbanded. Boys were still being birched for absconding. One boy who absconded twice was sent to an industrial training school.

In September 1903 extra snuff and tobacco was provided for inmates doing the more unpleasant jobs, such as emptying the ashpits (a primitive form of outdoor lavatory), cleaning drains

26

and working in the piggeries. However, because of rising costs, tobacco and snuff allowances for other inmates, except for the aged, were discontinued. One can imagine the bargaining that must have gone on among the inmates to get a 'drag' or 'sniff'! Mr Tonge again objected to the amount of liquor that the Medical Officer was giving to inmates for 'medication'. He said that Medical Officers in other parts of the country were coming to realise that whisky and brandy were not as beneficial a medication as was first thought.

At the next Workhouse Committee meeting, in October, the Medical Officer, Dr Buck, was called upon to make a statement about the use of alcohol. He said that whisky, used as a stimulant, was cheaper than brandy. It was only supplied from the stores on his orders, to the dispenser, who gave it as a drug. In Dr Buck's opinion, alcohol was used as a drug in the best hospitals in the world and it was given in this hospital only as a treatment for disease. He said that the consumption had increased in the previous year to 7/6d per head, due to more serious cases. Many people entered the Workhouse because of an alcohol problem, and the Medical Officer had always kept this fact in mind before prescribing. This explanation was accepted by most of the Guardians, though some still doubted the wisdom of such use of alcohol.

Still on the subject of alcohol, in 1904 a local businessman offered a gift of two barrels of beer for the inmates' Christmas Dinner. The offer was declined with thanks by the Committee, as no beer had been allowed for the past six years, even for the Christmas festivities. Some Guardians said it would be 'putting the clock back' if beer was again allowed, and it would be an encouragement for some inmates to start drinking again, as they had come to the Workhouse originally in a state of inebriation.

In May 1904 the Workhouse management was complimented when an inspector from the Government Board visited. He seemed pleased and satisfied that the institution was being run well. This in spite of the fact that just before his visit two male inmates absconded with Union clothing and damaged it! At this time, too, a female inmate named McNulty was sent to prison for the second time for brawling during the Roman Catholic Service in the Workhouse Chapel.

The inspector advised that children should be removed from the Workhouse when possible. This was not done until a later date, when more room became available at the cottage homes. Children under four years were not moved until the 1930s.

In August 1904 there was a re-classification of female inmates. Twelve ladies aged from 71 to 92 years, and 37 blind were placed in the 'first class' department. There were two classes of inmates at this time. First class had certain privileges on account of good conduct and age. Second class were 'low class' individuals; badly behaved and perhaps ignorant.

27

Pauperism in 1904 was increasing. There were 100 more admissions than in the corresponding period in 1903. The number of people living outside in receipt of relief – financial and material – had also gone up by 500. Local trade at this time was bad, especially in the cotton industry. Another reason for admissions to the Workhouse was that an increasing number of fathers or mothers were habitually neglecting their children. As they were sent to prison for this, the remaining family was put in the Workhouse. So it wasn't always lack of money in the first instance that caused families to be admitted.

All this put extra pressure on staff at Fishpool, and space had to be found for extra beds for families.

In 1905 all able-bodied men in the town on outdoor relief were put to work in the Workhouse grounds, tilling the soil, clearing paths, weeding the gardens and so on. This was said to be more character-building than chopping firewood at the casual wards alongside tramps.

In July 1905 two members of staff were sacked, the laundress for stealing starch and a nurse for stealing Bovril. In August, the laundress was replaced by one Maria Brooks, who later married the assistant cook, George Scholes. They both had residential appointments, and lived at the bungalow (previously the infectious diseases hospital and now the College of Nursing building) next door to us until the 1930s, when they both retired.

The Master, Mr Booth (Mr and Mrs Ratherham had left after only a short time, owing to Mrs Ratheram's ill health), decided to make a bowling green at the top of the grounds without consulting the Guardians. At their meeting they said the green was too near the infectious diseases hospital (the bungalow), but it was allowed to remain, and is still there. In the 1940s and 1950s the green was used by the staff for social club bowling matches.

Mr Booth also changed the dinner menus at this time:
Potato pie on Mondays (instead of boiled beef) for able-bodied men and women.
Sea pie on Wednesdays (instead of potato pie).
Suet pudding (instead of potato pie) for children aged 3-16.
Abolition of potato pie on Fridays, in favour of fish.

One Moses Waddington, an inmate, was buried as a pauper in the Workhouse Cemetery. Unknown to the Guardians, he had been awarded the sum of £5 from the Royal Ancient Order of Buffaloes, Nelson Lodge, to pay for his burial, and he also received £5 from Prudential Assurance. Moses had used £5 to buy clothes for his family before entering the Workhouse, and he gave the other £5 to his son for his burial. The son had spent the money on clothes instead of handing it in. The officials of Nelson Lodge wanted the couple exposed, which they were. The Guardians decided that in future they would check for any finance, insurance or burial club money before inmates were buried in the cemetery.

By December 1905 the female block for the sick was woefully overcrowded - 238 patients instead of 182, with 56 sleeping on the floor, and children two to a bed. The staff had put up four extra beds in a separate room for inmates who were suffering from tuberculosis, the infectious diseases block being full as well. The overcrowding was becoming a scandal and so a special committee was set up to consider the problem.

In spite of the difficulties, Christmas entertainment for 'well' inmates continued, and that year a concert party from Tonge Moor Wesleyan Church entertained.

In 1907 the overcrowding problem had not gone away and Dr Buck refused to discharge ill patients, as they would return again in a few days because they were not cured. He was working very hard, and since he was appointed Medical Officer twelve years previously, he had stood up to the Guardians, determined that conditions for the sick should improve. Before he came to the hospital the conditions were appalling. Untrained nurses were being paid the salary for qualified staff. There was no-one to teach nurses the procedures for looking after patients, no medication, and paupers helped on the wards - and charged for their services. Some patients who were admitted dirty and verminous remained so. Those that were reasonably clean on admission easily became verminous, because there was no attempt to rid the patients and wards of the problem.

*Christmas Dinner at Fishpool, 1920*

For his good work Dr Buck's salary was increased by £100 and furnished accommodation was provided. An Assistant Medical Officer, who also lived in, was appointed to help him.

In June 1907 proposed improvements at Fishpool included two new Lancashire boilers, a new stores, bakehouse and cookhouse. A new laundry was also needed, but this did not materialise until much later.

After Christmas 1907 there was an increase in the number of pregnant girls coming into the Workhouse. These were unlike the vagrants and paupers, and in all probability had been banished from their family homes on becoming pregnant. It was decided to appoint a Nurse Superintendent who possessed a midwifery qualification of the Central Midwives' Board. 52 nurses applied for this position.

Since 1861 (the year Fishpool Workhouse opened) there had been many attempts nationally to alter and improve conditions:

1862. The Poor Law 'Certified School Act' permitted Boards of Guardians to send children to institutions for the blind, deaf and dumb, and other special schools.
1870. Commencement of boarding of pauper children with foster parents.
1871. Provision of casual wards for vagrants.
      Establishment of training ships for poor law boys.
1879. Powers given to the Boards of Guardians to subscribe to voluntary hospitals (such as Bolton Royal Infirmary), Nursing Associations and institutions likely to render aid to persons in receipt of Poor Law relief.
1886. The provision of work for unemployed, without dis-franchisement.
1889. Statutory powers were given to the Guardians to take children from the control of parents who were unfit to look after them, or deserted them, by reason of vicious habits and mode of life.
1890. The commencement of further extensive improvements to Poor Law infirmaries.
1895. An increase in nursing staff of workhouse sick wards.
1896. Extended classification in workhouse of deserving and un-deserving poor.
1897. The practice of using workhouse inmates to help in nursing the sick and poor within the institution was abolished. Skilled nurses were to be employed instead, although in some institutions nurses were not always as skilled as they were supposed to be. (This was going on at Fishpool until stopped by Dr Buck.)
1900. Further classification of inmates, and more adequate relief to the aged.
1908. Old Age Pension Act - resulting in increased relief being given to aged poor living in their own homes, who had hitherto been disqualified by Parliament from participating

in the Old Age Pension scheme because they were receiving Poor Law relief.

In 1908 a Pensions Committee was formed in Bolton, as in many other towns, and the Board of Guardians were keen to be represented on it. The Committee proposed that monetary relief be increased to 5/- per week for poor people, but as one member of the Guardians said, 'How many outside the Work-house, aged 70 years and over, had any relief at all?'

# The Royal Commission and Social Changes

In 1909 a Royal Commission on Health and Social Services suggested that:

1. There should be abolition of general workhouses and Boards of Guardians.
2. There should be separate treatments for the aged and weak, able-bodied unemployed and the 'loafers'.
3. Vagrants should be sent to the Colonies.

New 'machinery' was proposed:

(a) One unit of administration for the county or county borough, instead of the Union.
(b) The Board of Guardians to be replaced by Public Assistance Authorities for central administration.
(c) A Public Assistance Committee to be appointed for dealing with applications for relief, together with Councils of Voluntary Aid, and various Sub-Committees to organise charities of an area under a Charity Commission.
(d) The Public Assistance Authority was to be the Statutory Committee of County and County Borough Councils, half of the members to belong to the local Council and half to be appointed by Councils outside: these to be nominated by Urban and Rural District Councils.
(e) The status of high local government officers was to be raised, with much greater care taken in selection of officials. The salaries offered must be adequate to men with powers of organisation and high moral qualities.
(f) No children were to be left in the Workhouse, even when these later became 'institutions'.
(g) Other systems of maintenance were to be approved, includ-ing emigration, and renewed supervision was to be exercised over outdoor relief for children outside the Workhouse.

The Board of Guardians at Fishpool discussed moving the children, as recommended by the Commission. If the children were removed from Fishpool it would mean that they would be placed in scattered homes, whereas at that time they were at least in a group home with people they knew. On the other hand, it was argued, the children should be moved to make more room for adult inmates. For the time being nothing was done and they turned their attention to normal domestic routine.

That year Dr Henn, the Vicar of Bolton and Chaplain to the Workhouse, became the Bishop of Burnley. The Guardians appointed Rev Pugh, Vicar of St James's, New Bury, as his successor at a salary of £70 per annum.

In 1910 a dog was bought for the Nurses' Home; the licence was paid for by the Master out of petty cash. Presumably Rover was intended as a companion and guard dog for the nurses.

Special permission had to be sought to enable children of resident officers to live in with them. The case of the married cook's children was discussed by the Workhouse Committee at this time. The cook's quarters were in the main house, and it was thought inadvisable for officers' children to live near the inmates. However, it was decided to allow the cook's children to live in, on payment of 5/- per week per child towards their keep.

In the days before time-saving sliced bread could be bought from outside bakeries, all the bread, cakes and pies were made on the premises, and in 1910 Mr J T Radcliffe, the baker, received an increase in pay from £84/10s to £93/12s per year. Mr W Radcliffe succeeded his father as baker.

The same year Mr Higham, a member of the Board of Guardians, conducted a party of prominent Bolton people through the Workhouse and to see new entrance gates, which were operated by hydraulic power from within the new lodge gates office. As well as touring all departments, the visitors saw the increased number of green-houses which provided flowers and plants to brighten up the day rooms. Other visitors to the Workhouse included a party of young ladies from a nursing class in Kearsley. They came to see nursing procedures carried out and were, presumably, from a St John's Ambulance or Red Cross class.

Later in 1910 it was decided to build an extension on to the main building and to transfer sick males to a new block of the hospital that was to become Townleys, so making room for more able-bodied inmates.

At this time the Workhouse was being used as a detention centre for juveniles, under the Children's Act of 1908. There was great objection to the scheme by the people of Bolton, and a special centre was set up later for these youngsters.

It was once again suggested that the Workhouse children be removed to make more room for elderly people, especially with winter coming. It was decided to let them remain because they would be looked after much better in the Workhouse than by poor and neglectful parents. However, it was possible to board out older children from the Cottage Homes, making some room for inmates in the vacated cottages.

In spite of all the overcrowding, the Board of Guardians were under pressure from other Boards, notably West Derby (Liverpool), to support a change in the law to empower Guardians to detain feeble-minded inmates within the safety of the Workhouse. It would protect them from danger and eliminate unwanted pregnancies.

In September 1910 a woman took the unusual step of writing a letter of gratitude. Her husband was in the Workhouse because he had no work, and she was receiving relief to help her keep the home going. She wrote to the Board of Guardians:

*'Kindly excuse the liberty I am taking in writing, but I consider it only right that I should acknowledge the very great kindness and courtesy you have shown to myself and my child, especially the gentlemen who went to such a lot of trouble to get relief (money) for me. I can only express my deepest gratitude. Again apologising for the liberty I have taken.*

*PS. I may here say you will never be able to estimate the very great help the relief has been to us, combined with the kindly manner in which it has been given.'*

Whilst in the Workhouse it was possible that the lady's husband was retrained for a different trade before returning home to a job. This was a way of preventing families breaking up because of poverty. Quite a few families were helped in this way, but it was most unusual for the Guardians to receive a letter of thanks.

By January 1911 it was thought that some of the more able inmates might wish to go and live in the community, helped by the new Old Age Pension award of 5/- per week. However, most wanted to stay in the Workhouse. They preferred comfort, cleanliness, reasonable food and freedom from worry to struggling to live outside in poor conditions. Even if the pension was doubled, there would always be some inmates who wanted to stay in the Workhouse, and there was always the fact that relatives did not want them, or could not afford to help to keep them.

Efforts to make room for the increasing number of sick and poor were still being made during 1911. Townleys' hospital blocks were extended to provide for 128 males. The number of beds in the wards for tuberculosis patients was increased to 64 each for males and females.

Young children were still in the Workhouse, but were moved to an area of their own away from the inmates, and were also under a separate administration, with a special Nursing Sister with her own staff. Ordinary inmates were placed together in the main building, and sick inmates put together in the block which is now Russell Vickers. Moving patients and inmates around eliminated the need for using the cottage homes for adults, as was planned earlier. This meant that the children could remain in the Homes, and a boundary wall was built round the cottages to separate them from the Workhouse, with a separate entrance from Plodder Lane. In later years a special path or 'ginnel' was made around the perimeter of the Workhouse grounds, so that when the children went to ordinary schools (Plodder Lane Council School, St Simon's & St Jude's Schools being two of them) they could get to the homes without having to go through the Workhouse grounds.

In 1911 the Coronation of King George V was celebrated with tea parties, brass bands and entertainment by local concert parties. Colourful bunting decorated the grounds, Union Jacks were hoisted and small flags were given to children and inmates to wave.

During this Coronation Year Mr Booth, the Master, died suddenly. He and Mrs Booth had been Master and Matron since 1901, but his death meant that Mrs Booth had to leave her job, losing her accommodation. This system continued until the 1960s and was the rule in most Authorities. The couple appointed to succeed the Booths were Mr and Mrs W R P Burns. The salary was £200 per annum, with £150 allowed for food and accommodation.

Later that year a young man, Mr J J Farrell from Wigan, was appointed (non-resident) assistant book-keeper at £85 per year. In later years he was promoted to Townleys Hospital Steward (the forerunner of Hospital Secretary, now Manager).

An epidemic of ringworm of the scalp occurred among the young children and babies in the nursery. The infection was said to have been brought into the building by two infants who were transferred from another home. To deal with the problem and treat the children two special nurses were appointed at £35 per year, with uniform, board and lodgings provided.

*Children at Hollins Cottage Homes, 1927*

A new block for 'harmless lunatics' was proposed in 1911 but this was not built as money was needed elsewhere. I believe that at a later date the blocks that housed the male and female sick wards were extended at either end to accommodate the mentally afflicted. Other expenses that year included the purchase of X-Ray machines for the part of Townleys that was then built (possibly A and B blocks). £28,000 was needed for more cottages at the cottage homes. At that time there were only 22 places for older children in Bolton, whereas Salford had 259 places. So it was necessary to increase accommodation for children needing care.

On the social side, a soccer team was founded in November 1911 by staff at Fishpool, and they played a team in West Manchester - the score is not recorded. Around Christmas the Farnworth Male Voice Choir gave a concert for the inmates.

The new Master, Mr Burns, was keen to exercise more discipline, particularly in the laundry. Working routines here had become lax, mainly because inmates provided unpaid help. The Master asked for, and got, extra paid help.

Ringworm was still a problem in 1912. The disease was causing a lot of worry - even the Workhouse cats were destroyed because they were considered to be the cause of the infection.

The rest of the Townleys Hospital blocks were completed towards the end of 1913 and plans were made to transfer patients from the old Male Infirmary to the new hospital. This would allow the old block to be used for tramps, and would provide 200 beds. (The old Male Infirmary was demolished in the 1930s and was on the site presently occupied by the Engineering works and Maintenance departments. I remember seeing the tramps come and go from this building, and men working on the gardens as payment for a night's shelter before being allowed to go on their way.)

In 1913 something had to be done to segregate the tramps from the resident inmates and main building because of alleged pilfering of food and general bad behaviour by the tramps. These tramps were classified as 'able-bodied undeserving'. The number of women tramps was increasing - 580 in 1912. Two extra attendants were appointed to work in the new tramp ward, and the two charge nurses' salaries were increased from £30/£32 to £34/£36 per annum.

Tramps were usually admitted on a strict time basis. 9.00pm was the deadline for a night's sleep and food, and they were out on the road again about 10.00am, after carrying out various chores. However, in January 1913 men and women of the road were being admitted at other times: 9.00pm-10.00pm, 46 males and 6 females; 10.00pm-11.00pm, 32 males and 11 females; after 11.00pm, 9 males and 4 females. Two females were even admitted

# BOLTON UNION.

## Scale of Rations for Officers and Servants of the Workhouse.

### (EXCEPT THE MASTER AND MATRON).

| ARTICLES. | Weekly Quantities Each. |
|---|---|
| Meat (uncooked, including bone) ... ... ... ... ... ... | ‡ 6 lbs. |
| Bacon ... ... ... ... ... ... ... ... ... | ¾ lb. |
| Eggs ... ... ... ... ... ... ... ... ... | 6 |
| Butter ... ... ... ... ... ... ... ... ... | 14 ozs. |
| Sugar { Lump ... ... ... ... ... ... ... ... | ¾ lb. |
| Sugar { Moist ... ... ... ... ... ... ... ... | 1 lb. |
| Potatoes ... ... ... ... ... ... ... ... ... | 7 lbs. |
| Cheese ... ... ... ... ... ... ... ... ... | ½ lb. |
| Jam, Marmalade or Syrup, divided as required ... ... ... ... | ½ lb. |
| Tea, Coffee or Cocoa, divided as required ... ... ... ... | 8 ozs. |
| Flour ... ... ... ... ... ... ... ... ... | 6¼ lbs. |
| Lard, Suet or Margarine ... ... ... ... ... ... ... | ¼ lb. |
| Milk ... ... ... ... ... ... ... ... ... ... | 7 pts. |
| Raisins, Currants or Candied Peel ... ... ... ... ... ... | 4 ozs. |
| Rice, Sago, Tapioca, Cornflour, Macaroni, Ground Rice or Packet Jellies to the same value | ½ lb. |
| Fruit and Vegetables ... ... ... ... ... ... ... | value ‖ 6d. |
| Pickles, Sauces, Spices and Flavouring Essences ... ... ... ... | as required |
| Barley, Lentils, Peas, Beans and Oatmeal, divided as required ... ... | ¼ lb. |
| Aerated Waters (various) ... in lieu of value of 2 pints of milk weekly as required | |
| Vinegar, Salt, Mustard and Pepper ... ... ... ... ... ... | as required |

‡ Meat to include beef, mutton, fish, pork, lamb, tongue, tripe, liver, kidney and veal in season. Quarter of chicken or duck in lieu of 1 lb. of meat, or 1 rabbit in lieu of 2 lbs. of meat once weekly. Fish to include fresh fish in season, dried fish twice weekly.

‖ Fruit to include fresh fruit in season, canned or bottled and dried fruit such as prunes and figs, &c.

The above scale represents the maximum allowance, and does not authorise any officer to demand the quantities set forth unless required for actual consumption, and all unconsumed provisions must be returned to the Stores.

Adopted by the Workhouse Committee on the 15th October, 1913, and approved by the Guardians on the 22nd October, 1913.

### H. I. COOPER,
#### Clerk to the Guardians.

28, MAWDSLEY STREET, BOLTON,
22nd October, 1913.

after 2.00am. It was alleged that this was due to inefficiency and mis-management of the tramp ward.

Tramps were not going on their way the following day, and strict routine was not being followed. It was said by the Workhouse Committee, and other people involved with the running of the institution, that the casual ward was becoming a 'second workhouse' because of these irregularities.

At this time 16 'undeserving' inmates were moved to a ward of their own. One of the male blocks was adapted at a cost of £100 to separate these men from ordinary inmates, as their rough behaviour made them difficult to manage in the main Workhouse.

The new Townleys, Hospital was opened to the public on 9th and 12th April 1913 as part of the activities for a 'National Health Week'. On 10th July, on the occasion of the visit to Bolton by King George V and Queen Mary, the Workhouse children were invited to join in the festivities.

In October, Workhouse extensions were planned, these to include a new provisions store, bakehouse, cookhouse, boilerhouse and chip-cutting shop, where old trees were cut up and made into bundles of firewood by the inmates for selling. A shoe repair shop and tailors' shop were also planned. All these buildings were erected on the road opposite the present Russell Vickers ward; the bakehouse is now the stationery department. The last tailor was Mr Fray.

With a few exceptions, staff at the Workhouse were resident at this time. On 22nd October 1913 the scale of food allowances was circulated. The quantity of food each individual received was arrived at mainly by the efforts of Mr Burns. Even during the Great War, food allowances did not vary a great deal, although the weekly meat ration was reduced from 6 lb in 1913 to $2\frac{1}{2}$ lb in 1917.

22nd October 1913 was also the 101st birthday of one of the inmates, Mrs Ruth Turner. Mrs Turner's mother and father emigrated to Canada after their marriage, but for some reason decided to return to England. Mrs Turner was born on the return crossing and the family settled in Nantwich, Cheshire, where she was brought up; they later moved to Sheffield. She met and married Mr Turner, a Bolton man who was a carrier with Walker's Tannery. They had three children, who all died from smallpox in the same week. After her husband's death Mrs Turner lived on what money she had saved, and then she went 'hawking' (door-to-door selling). When that became too much for her she entered the Workhouse at the age of 85 years in 1897. At 101, her memory was good; she could hear all that was said and only wore spectacles for reading. She arose at six o'clock each morning and made her own bed. For her birthday celebration a lady member of the Board of Guardians made a cake. Mrs Turner's only wish was that a visiting band should play the hymn 'There is a fountain filled with blood', whilst the inmates and staff sang. She remembered her mother singing the hymn to her when she was a small child.

This grand old lady died on 2nd June 1914 and was buried in Tonge Cemetery, which at that time had been made available for inmates at Fishpool.

In December 1913 it was decided to adapt the old male infirmary for use by 'harmless lunatics', but by April 1914 this had not been done and the work was deferred for six months. This adaptation was necessary because other hospitals in the North of England were housing 950 lunatics from Bolton and district, all chargeable to Bolton at the rate of approximately 14/- per head per week. The mental patients were moved to their own block in 1915, when padded rooms were built into the refurbished male infirmary (now Russell Vickers).

Until 1914 the staff could freely use mechanical restraints to prevent lunatics from injuring themselves or others. However, in that year such restraints were to be used only in emergency and with the approval of the Medical Officer. The cupboard housing the appliances was to be kept locked, and there were only two keys - one with the Medical Officer and the other in the Master's office. (This key remained in the Master's office until reorganisation in 1948 although, of course, it was never used in later times.) In 1925 there were new regulations on restraint of patients: mechanical means were limited to a strait jacket of strong linen and gloves without fingers. Patients likely to injure themselves were also placed in a padded room - a small room completely lined with covered foam rubber from floor to ceiling, and with a 'spy hole' for observation in the heavy, padded door.

In January 1914 Mr and Mrs Brand, Master and Matron from Derby Cottage Homes, were appointed to run the cottage homes at Fishpool at salaries of £85 and £45 per year. Older children still at the Workhouse were to be removed to these homes, 15 to each house, when new buildings were ready. There were already 45 children, aged 3 to 16 years, in the old houses. There were foster mothers, two or three to each house, and the children had a separate Medical Officer.

By the end of 1914 the last of the children's homes had been built. Unfortunately, the Great War had started and military nurses from Townleys Hospital were accommodated in these new cottages. By 1916 the complex had been named Hollins Cottage Homes, separated from the Workhouse by a boundary wall. The original school had become a small hospital for minor ailments, the nurses were housed elsewhere and the cottages were occupied by the children as originally intended. By this time they wore ordinary clothing so that when they attended local schools they were indistinguishable from the other children. Girl Guide and

Boy Scout companies were formed within the Homes. All these improvements gave the children more enjoyment in life – human affection and childish joys that 'Bumbledom' had denied them.

When the boys were 14 years old they were sent to a working boys' hostel in Arkwright Street; the girls remained at the Homes for domestic training to prepare some of them for life as resident domestic helps in large houses. Today the Homes belong to the Bolton Housing Department, and are used for Homeless Family Units.

# The Great War Years

During the Great War the whole establishment – the new Townleys and the old Workhouse – was involved in the war effort. In 1914 the Guardians gave permission for local units of the voluntary organisations (St John Ambulance and British Red Cross Society) to observe nursing procedures, treatment of wounds and bandaging. This was so that members could be ready to help in the hospital when wounded soldiers were admitted to the new blocks. The first wounded arrived in January 1915. In March, 30 more wounded came in. Patients were moved over to Fishpool from the new Townleys to make room for the increasing number of soldiers. Colonel Coates, the local Commanding Officer, asked for all 225 beds of Townleys to be available for wounded soldiers, with nursing to be carried out by army nurses and medical orderlies. More wounded were expected by July, and to make room for these some inmates were moved to Chorley Workhouse and Lake Hospital, Ashton-under-Lyne.

Spending was curtailed during the war and work such as road and path improvements was postponed. Staffing, however, was not cut, and extra male attendants were employed; there were 129 applications for two posts. An Assistant Superintendent Nurse was appointed at Townleys to supervise nurses and train probationer nurses. In the same year a Matron, Miss Holland, was appointed, and so was a Home Sister, Miss Wood, to look after the nurses living in the Nurses' Home. Both these ladies remained in their posts for many years until retirement.

Mr Burns, the Master, applied for permission to join the army, but was refused because the presence of wounded soldiers on the premises classed him as exempt from military service. In spite of the war, Mr Burns succeeded in improving the diet of both patients and staff. The nurses' butter ration was supplemented by margarine, and 36 signed a petition protesting about this. The margarine continued to be used.

Visits to wounded soldiers by relatives were strictly controlled and only two tickets per soldier were allowed. These tickets were obtained from the Medical Officer; the soldier sent the tickets to his relatives, who then had to present themselves with the tickets to the Porter at the gates. Visiting was only on

Wednesdays, Saturdays and Sundays, from 2.00pm to 4.30pm, except, of course, for emergencies.

Towards the end of 1915 Workhouse nurses protested about the differences in pay and staffing between local and army nurses. Local nurses wanted their salary increasing to £50 per year, plus the opportunity to become military nurses. The staffing position on the military side was much better, there being 12 charge nurses and 25 female staff nurses, as well as junior staff for 200 male patients. As a result of the protest, Workhouse nurses' salaries were increased by £5 to £45 (to £50 for the night sister) for the duration of the war.

By August 1916 the number of wounded soldiers had increased to 493, due to 'the push in Flanders'. Tributes to nurses in war work came from various sources in the town. For army nurses on night duty, room to sleep during the day was scarce. The old, single-storey infectious diseases hospital was brought into use for them, but only after the verandah had been filled in with wood and glass – to make the building secure, it was said, from visiting soldiers. This alteration cost £119/18/6d and accommodated 17 nurses.

*Townleys at Christmas 1918. Reproduced with the kind permission of Mrs Wolfendale, whose mother (in white, at front) was a voluntary worker*

40

Another problem with the soldiers was that some of them climbed over the institution wall to meet female workers. This was frowned upon by the Committee, who asked for adequate supervision of convalescent soldiers. Huts on the lawn were provided by the YMCA so that soldiers could sit and have peace and quiet. In order to alleviate depression suffered by some of the soldiers, a recreation pavilion was provided by Mrs Knowles-Edge.

In 1917 the Medical Officer, Dr Buck, retired after 25 years' service. His place was taken by a military Medical Officer until 1919.

The number of inmates in the Workhouse was steadily decreasing - in 1912 there were 1,282, in 1917 there were 632. There was practically no poverty in the town at this time. People were enjoying prosperity, and those who had previously been at the mercy of the Union, and consequently the Workhouse, due to slackness in trade, were well able to maintain themselves. It was just as well there were fewer inmates, because in May 1917 the number of wounded soldiers was 620, and five tents had to be erected in the grounds for 60 additional wounded.

Early in 1917 two men were engaged to assist in cultivation and keep the grounds in order; women were employed in cultivating flowers. Some of the Guardians thought that they would be better employed in growing food as there was a war on, but others thought that the flowers should be grown to adorn the hospital and gladden the hearts of the wounded soldiers and other patients.

Until 1917 medicines and drugs had come from local chemists, instead of direct from the wholesale firms such as Burroughs Wellcome and Parke Davis. In the September of that year a dispenser, Margaret Martin, was appointed to distribute medicines to the wards and departments. Miss Martin originally lived in Manchester Road, but in the 1930s she lived at the old gatehouse on Greenland Road (previously Wash Lane) which had led to Townleys House, the working boys' and girls' hostel. Miss Martin succeeded Miss Taylor, who had been appointed in 1908.

In 1917 casual wards for tramps were closed at other workhouses in the North West, such as Bury, Leigh, Oldham and Rochdale, and Fishpool had to bear the burden of extra tramps. One of the old infirmary blocks (now demolished) was brought into use for them.

The Workhouse Engineer had retired in 1916 and was not replaced until 1917, when Walter Rushton, my grandfather, was appointed. In October the Master and Matron's salary was increased from £120 to £150. The number of inmates had dropped by half and nursing staff was reduced, but the increase was agreed because of Mr and Mrs Burns' conscientious work and industrious application to duties.

An assistant superintendent nurse was dispensed with, as were three male attendants. The number of nurses in the hospital was fixed at one nurse to eight patients, including male infirm patients (elderly chronic sick), day and night.

In June 1918 the Brabazon Society (Ladies' Section) supplied a long carriage wheelchair so that wounded soldiers could be wheeled out into the fresh air. The Society also supplied various board games for recreation.

In 1919 Dr E Spencer Miller was appointed Medical Superintendent and Dr Lucy Kelleher his Assistant. In that year it was decided that the new Townleys Hospital should be managed separately from Fishpool Workhouse. It could then be used by the rate-payers of Bolton, who helped to bear the expense of its upkeep. 150 beds were made available, and a separate path from that leading to the Workhouse was made, so that sick people could go into the hospital without suffering the pauper stigma.

*The Board of Guardians in 1919. Third from the right on the middle row is T W Gorringe. Standing in the doorway is W R P Burns, the Master. Seated on the ground, centre, is H I Cooper, Clerk to the Guardians*                    *(Courtesy Miss S Gorringe)*

The provision of beds at Townleys helped to relieve overcrowding at Bolton Royal Infirmary, for which there was a long waiting list.

From the start there was resistance among the populace to being sent to Townleys. When a doctor suggested to one of his patients that he should be treated there, the reply was, 'But that's the Workhouse. Surely you don't mean that place?' The Bolton Journal & Guardian of 29th August 1919 commented: 'No doubt this reply will occur many times in the future.' This attitude was often to be found among the elderly sick well into the 1950s, 60s and 70s.

## Post War Changes

Eventually 500 beds were made available at Townleys for ordinary sick people. The new wards were light and airy, well separated, with bays opening out into balconies. The present connecting corridors had not been built at this time. The operating theatre (then on C Block) was the most modern in the country. Patients had the privilege of being operated on by the doctor of their choice, at the patients' expense. Otherwise, the inclusive charge for hospital care was two guineas per week. One happy patient said it was 'Beyond my expectations', after going home quite recovered.

The fact that Townleys Hospital was still administered by the Guardians, but managed separately from the Workhouse, was of great interest to the rest of the country's workhouse administrators, being a unique scheme. A gentleman who had been a private patient in Townleys wrote to the Bolton Evening News on 23rd September 1919:

'...I feel it is my duty to let the public know that the treatment I received was all that could be desired. The equipment for all classes of cases compares with any hospital in the country. There are two operating theatres, X-Ray room, with all the latest appliances. The Guardians can be complimented upon the recent appointment of Dr Miller and his assistant Dr Kelleher, both having the best qualifications and experience of institution life. Private patients can also have their own Doctor visiting, so anyone can rest assured of having the best medical and surgical treatment; also skilful nursing. Another great feature is the healthy situation of Townleys. Its grounds and open spaces are well laid out, and afford ample recreation for convalescent patients...*

*Fred Morris, Strawberry Hill Road.'*

Back at the Workhouse, 30 male and 30 female mental defectives, together with 25 'harmless lunatics' were being housed in the block vacated by the male sick when they were moved to the new hospital in November 1919.

Pocket money for inmates was unheard of as yet. Mr Burns applied to the Ministry of Health to obtain this precedent, not only for Fishpool but for other institutions. He suggested an amount not exceeding 5/- per year, and inmates not to have more than 1/3d at any one time. The Ministry turned down the application, owing to the expensive aftermath of the war.

Some Workhouse equipment, such as that in the old laundry, was getting the worse for wear. Because the machinery kept breaking down, there was disappointment for eight little girls at the Workhouse. They were to be 'Little Singers' at St James' (New Bury) Sermons, and special white dresses were sent back from the laundry still dirty. These dresses had been worn the day previously by eight Roman Catholic girls in their procession, and had got soiled. Clothes for special occasions in those days had to be shared. It was not until seven years later that a new laundry was built.

A connecting corridor was needed between new wards at Townleys, to protect staff walking to the various departments in inclement weather. However, there was a delay because brick-layers were badly needed in the town for building new houses and replacing those destroyed by bombs. In 1921 the building of the new corridor was delayed again because tenders for the work were judged to be too high.

Beds were still vacant at Townleys, although there was a waiting list at Bolton Royal Infirmary of 5-6 weeks. The 'Poor Law' stigma was still strong. In June 1921 private patients' fees were increased to 7/6d per day. The average weekly cost was £2/8/3d, which was cheaper than the Manchester hospitals, whose fees were three guineas a week.

Good standards of nursing were maintained by the introduction of proper training for nurses. It was agreed with the General Nursing Council for England and Wales that Townleys should have a nursing school. So in 1922 a Sister Tutor was appointed at a salary of £100 per year, with keep and uniform.

In 1923 plans were submitted for an administrative block, maternity block, nurses' home extension and the new laundry at Fishpool. There were also to be extensions to the boilerhouse and a calorifier house.

In October 1923 permission was given for female inmates to have two ounces of sweets per week.

In 1924 the Medical Superintendent was given permission to accept fees for consultancy work, provided it did not interfere with hospital duties. The Workhouse Committee thought that the experience would benefit the hospital and the institution.

Later in 1924, blood was urgently needed to save the life of a patient at Townleys. An inmate of the institution volunteered to give blood and was paid 5/-. This was a lot of money to an

44

inmate, who did not get much chance to make 'extra'. Apparently the giving of blood for payment was quite a common occurrence in other institutions, but this was the first, and only, time it had taken place at Fishpool.

## Segregation and Improvements

In August 1924 a journalist from the Bolton Journal & Guardian visited Fishpool to see how conditions had improved over the years. Inmates were segregated in the Probationary Ward (Admissions). Those with bad habits were separated from the more congenial inmates. *'Gone are the days when all inmates, irrespective of class, were herded together.'* The journalist saw First and Second Class dormitories and sitting rooms, which were comfortable, light and spacious. The bedrooms had lockers and bedside mats, and the sitting rooms had armchairs, chenille cloths and flowers on the tables, and pictures on the walls. There was a cosy atmosphere, with fires burning brightly, and inmates chatting together about old times, doing needlework or reading. Younger inmates were in the workrooms, making new

*Invalid inmates around the central stove in the Men's Ward at Townleys Hospital, 1920*

garments or darning socks and stockings. There was a well-furnished nursery for inmates' children. In the mental wards, he found that the inmates were actually talking to one another, not sitting about, depressed, as he had thought.

Towards the end of 1924 Dr Miller applied to live outside the Workhouse. This was readily agreed to, as the Workhouse atmosphere was considered undesirable for his children. The Assistant Medical Superintendent was already living in, so that was considered sufficient for 'on call' duties.

Christmas Dinner was much improved, with chicken and pork as well as the traditional roast beef. The Guardians of bygone years would have been amazed at the changes. The dining hall was decorated with evergreens, which provided an attractive background for bright flowers, flags and Chinese lanterns hung from the ceiling. Another important change was the introduction of smaller dining tables, instead of the very long ones running the width of the dining room. Chairs replaced backless benches. Mr Burns had fought for these changes, and they were early evidence of a gradual improvement in conditions.

360 inmates sat down to Christmas Dinner. The aged faces of the women were framed in snowy white bonnets; the younger female inmates wore little frilly caps. All wore bright red or plaid shawls. The men wore smart suits with collar and tie. Music was played on the organ, which at that time was on the balcony, whilst dinner was in progress. The Mayor, Councillor Steele, and the Mayoress, his sister Mrs Jones, attended the meal. In the afternoon, concert parties toured the various departments and in the evening there was a grand entertainment in the dining room, where a temporary stage had been erected. The women were given four ounces of sweets and the men two ounces of tobacco or ten cigarettes.

Early in 1925 electricity was supplied and the whole of Fishpool was lit by electric light instead of gas. The central heating from the boilers was extended and improved.

In April the first lady Chairman of the Guardians, Mrs Percy Knott JP, took office. In May, Mr Burns bought a motor car, but he had to apply to the Guardians for permission to garage it. In support of his application, it was said that he needed a car to get out and about in what off duty time he had, which was not very much.

The number of inmates for 1924/25 was 455; of these 88 were mentally infirm.

Foul wash from the sick wards had to be wheeled to the old laundry in all weather. This task was carried out by a 42-year-old inmate who was allowed an extra ounce of tobacco per week for doing this chore.

In December 1925 an inmate was seen taking food from one of the pig swill bins outside the kitchen. A complaint was made to the master and it was stated that the man was not getting enough to eat in the normal way. This allegation was refuted – the diet was quite adequate and it was unnecessary to steal food meant for the pigs. The daily cost per inmate for care worked out at 1/3d, including warmth, light, clothing and medicines, when necessary.

As a result of complaints, it was decided at a Guardians' meeting in January 1926 to make a wider variety of food available, including jam and marmalade. There was not a shortage of food; the changes were made to relieve the monotony of everyday meals.

The white caps worn by lady inmates were abolished at Christmas 1926, but shawls were still worn. Another change that was made this year was that resident inmates had the sole use of the Dining Hall for Christmas Dinner; previously they had had to share space with any vagrants who happened to find their way to the Workhouse on Boxing Day. The vagrants had their Christmas Dinner on the casual ward.

Visiting of inmates by ministers of religion became an issue at one Guardians' meeting. When Salvation Army officers and an official from an Independent Methodist Church had applied for permission to visit, one member said, 'If visiting by more religious bodies was allowed, they would be having seances in the wards before long.' His objections were considered exaggerated and unreasonable and the visits were allowed.

Bolton-based members of the Workhouse Committee had come under fire from the ratepayers some years earlier for using a private bus to take them to meetings at Fishpool. This practice was abandoned because of the expense. In 1926 the members travelled by tram to Rishton Lane and walked down the ginnel, the path running alongside the old railway line, from Rishton Avenue to the institution entrance. This, of course, was what everyone else who worked at or visited the Fishpool or Townleys buildings had to do at that time.

In November 1926 there was a ban on smoking in bed at Townleys because of the risk of fire. This followed a fatal accident to a patient who was smoking in bed. One member of the Workhouse Committee objected to the ban, 'because there are only three short periods allowed for smoking in any case. We all know, and it is generally admitted, that smoking soothes the nerves, and I believe to many a person who is ill, a smoke is of more benefit than the Doctor's medicine.' (There are very few today who would agree with that philosophy!)

## Townleys Hospital and Extensions

Christmas Dinner continued to improve and both Fishpool and Townleys benefitted from the changes. The dinner was cooked in Fishpool kitchens – the hospital kitchen at that time was not large enough. In 1926 1,000 patients and inmates were provided for and the dinner consisted of 900 lb of beef and pork, 1,000 lb of fresh vegetables, 630 lb of plum pudding and 480 lb of Christmas cake. In addition, 34 chickens were cooked for Townleys Hospital only - perhaps these were for the paying patients.

In his speech after the dinner, Mr E Wardle, Chairman of the Workhouse Committee, said that the work of the Guardians in the distant past had been mainly to the detriment of the wellbeing of inmates. In the last 20 years the Committee had tried to influence the staff to make their work remedial in looking after the inmates, 'and I think we are succeeding'. The work at Townleys Hospital bore testimony to the efforts of the Guardians. Extensions were being built - an administrative block, operating theatre and maternity block (E Ward) - and older blocks were being modernised; all this at a cost of £100,000.

Alderman Percy Knott, Deputy Mayor, whose wife was a member of the Board of Guardians, also spoke at the dinner and paid tribute to the hospital. 'There is now a nursing staff of 80, and no longer do patients die unattended. The Poor Law hospital is no longer a reproach. Whether you will be Guardians much longer or not, I do not know.' (He was referring to the proposal to abolish the Guardians.) 'It is all in the melting pot, but one thing I will say. I hope that the body which will succeed you will be equally sympathetic to the people under their care.'

In March 1927 an influenza epidemic hit both Townleys and Fishpool and there were shortages in all departments. However, good came out of the situation because unemployed people were taken on, temporarily, to fill vacancies created by sickness.

At this time men who could not, or would not, find work were given outdoor relief in return for doing casual work, mainly at Fishpool and Townleys. One of their tasks was to chop 'chips' for firewood and bundle them for sale. This was said to be degrading by some members of the Workhouse Committee, but the practice continued for some time. I remember an inmate being in charge of the 'chip shop' later in 1927.

*Walter Rushton, Engineer at Fishpool and Townleys 1917-36*

In April 1927 my father was appointed resident Assistant Engineer at Fishpool and Townleys. His father, Mr W Rushton, was the non-resident Foreman Engineer, appointed in 1917. Father's wages were 56/- for a 47-hour working week, and being resident meant that he was on call for emergencies. We were given accommodation in the Old Lodge, for which we paid 15/- per week, which included light, coal and water. Furniture and linen were also provided, but we had to use our own crockery, cutlery, cleaning and cooking utensils. We arrived at the lodge gates on a dull, rainy day in a borrowed car containing all our possessions. After we identified ourselves to the lodge porter, he unlocked the large iron gates by means of a large wheel inside the lodge office, and admitted us and the car into the grounds. Our first home at Fishpool was really too small for a family and it later became accommodation for successive Assistant Matrons. Today it is Flat 13, a residence for doctors.

In November 1927 Townleys nurses' hours were increased from 50 to 56 per week and annual salaries were increased by £5. The staffs of Manchester and Salford hospitals were already working 56 hours, and Townleys Committee thought that theirs should do the same. A charge nurse's (sister's) salary was £75 and other nurses were paid £35, as against the £10 for an 85-hour week 20 years earlier.

In January 1928 Dr Gawne, the Medical Superintendent appointed in 1926, was given permission to live out of the hospital grounds provided he had a telephone and a car in order to be

*Administrative Block, 1929*

on call. In the same month, Rev Hansford, Vicar of St James', New Bury, was appointed Chaplain to both Fishpool and Townleys at £100 per year. He succeeded the Rev Pugh, who had retired.

The annual report for 1927/28, compiled by the Medical Superintendent, showed good progress at Townleys. Following completion of the extensions, a new sunlight clinic for out-patients was planned. During the year, 3,041 Poor Law patients (who paid according to their means) and 140 private patients were admitted. 466 operations were performed. Of these, 59 were on private patients; 19 were carried out by hospital surgeons and 40 by the patients' own doctors. 522 patients were X-rayed and 127 received a total of 5,084 treatments in the massage

*Three Laundry workers: Miss Pennington, Mrs Maria Scholes (Laundress) and Miss Hill*

*The Laundry in 1929*

therapy department. 81 patients received 1,591 ultra-violet light sessions.

The extensions at Fishpool Institution, planned in 1923, were completed at this time. There was a new laundry, an extension to the boilerhouse to accommodate an additional steam boiler, and a calorifier house (now the linen room at the rear of the laundry). The boilerhouse extension was necessary to cope with extra central heating at Fishpool and for the whole of Townleys Hospital. It also provided hot water for the Nurses' Home, kitchens and operating theatre sterilizers.

Extensions at the hospital were on a much larger scale:
1. An operating block with theatre, anaesthetic and sterilizing rooms; Surgeons' and Nurses' rooms; Dental Department; Laboratory; X-Ray and dark rooms; Ultra-violet ray department; Massage and Remedial Exercises room; Eye and Ear rooms; Waiting rooms and offices. All these departments were built beyond and at the back of A Block.

2. An Administrative Block, which is still in use. At that time this also included quarters for the Matron, Assistant Matron and doctors, and a boardroom. At the rear of the block (now divided by the main corridor) was a kitchen, nurses' dining room (now an office) and Dispensary (still there). The maids' quarters were upstairs.

3. Maternity pavilion (E Block).

4. A corridor connecting all hospital blocks. It was 900 feet long and now, of course, it is even longer with an extension to the Princess Anne Maternity Unit.

5. A Nurses' Home extension, which included the sitting room, lecture rooms and additional bathrooms and lavatories.

The very first extensions were begun in 1898, with two blocks for the sick inmates at Fishpool. Over the years there had been gradual improvements, refurbishments and the building of the first blocks of Townleys. The total expenditure over these years had been £160,000. Management by the Board of Guardians was due to come to an end and on 1st February 1929 the Bolton Journal & Guardian paid this tribute:

'Whosoever may take charge of Townleys Hospital, on the dissolution of the Board, the Guardians have certainly accomplished, by its splendid development, a great service to the communal life of this area. For many years to come, the sick of Bolton and district will have cause to praise the foresight of the Board, in providing treatment on the most modern lines for all classes of people. It sounds expensive, but the rising generation will discover how effectively the Board launched out to keep pace with the needs of the future by means of the most modern equipment.'

With the completion of Townleys and improvements at the Workhouse, the 'pauper' taint was gradually being removed. As Mr H I Cooper, Clerk to the Board of Guardians, said, 'It takes all classes, rich and poor alike, just like a general hospital. Those who can afford it, of course, we charge the full rate, as private patients, at a cost of $2\frac{1}{2}$ guineas a week. If patients cannot afford to pay, we make no distinction.'

As a little girl of $4\frac{1}{2}$ years old I was getting used to living a life of my own in the institution grounds. At that time I was the only child of a residential officer living in. Mr and Mrs Burns, the Master and Matron, had a daughter, but she was much older and away at college. Mr and Mrs Burns were very good to me, and let me go into all the day rooms to see the old people, and into the nursery to play with the very young children (some of them children of inmates). The children had a magnificent leather-upholstered donkey cart which was regularly used for trips round the grounds and for a short distance outside. I was always invited along in my pre-school days. The old people appeared to be very happy and comfortable in their cosy day room with a cheerful coal fire. I made friends with the donkey man, the pig man and the man in charge of the 'chip shop'. All these were inmates, and there was no fear, then, of being harmed by the men. They were all my friends, along with a lady inmate called Emily, who came to help Father and me in the house and bring meals over from the kitchen when Mother was seriously ill in Townleys. The Attendants (later Assistant Nurses) also took an interest in me and some of them, particularly Miss Fahy, who hailed from the North East, and Miss Mayoh, used to buy me presents.

## Public Assistance Committee Takes Over

In 1930 the Poor Law Act which abolished the Board of Guardians was passed. On 26th March the Guardians had their last meeting, at which long service awards were presented to Mr Wardle, the Chairman, and Mrs Faith Holden. There was a balance of £23,000 in the funds and this was handed over to Bolton Corporation. The first meeting of the newly-formed Public Assistance Committee took place on 30th April.

Management of Townleys and Fishpool under the Public Assistance Committee seemed to run very smoothly. Indeed, when Miss Lawrence, Parliamentary Secretary to the Ministry of Health, visited later that year, she was most impressed with the work that was going on.

In spite of improvements in institutional care, outside help for young men with no work was difficult to obtain. Just before Christmas an ex-soldier was refused outdoor relief because he had not lived in the district (Turton) for one year. He was offered institutional relief – that is, living and doing odd jobs at Fishpool. He refused, saying, 'While I have these hands, I am not going in there'. Presumably the shock of the alternative forced him into finding work.

By this time I had started at St Simon and St Jude's Church of England School in Great Lever. To get there I had to walk down the ginnel and alongside the hospital farm and railway, a distance of about 1¼ miles, four times a day. (There were no school dinners then, and no transport). Each time I had to go through the turnstile at the lodge, as the large iron gates were kept locked except to admit cars, which were few and far between in those days. When I came home I would play in the grounds, talk to inmates or sometimes watch the trains from Great Moor Street Station on the line which ran alongside the hospital and crossed the bridge over Minerva Road (now demolished).

The work and problems of Townleys and Fishpool went on. Suddenly there was overcrowding at Townleys Hospital: 21 urgent admissions in one night. The committee decided to move 40 elderly women over to 'Infirm 2', the sick ward (now Dowling) at Fishpool. These patients were what used to be called chronic sick, and whilst they were given good care, it was unknown at that time to attempt to get them up for rehabilitation and physiotherapy.

*Infirm 1 (Females) in 1930. This is now Ernsting Ward*

At Fishpool inmates went to bed at 6.00pm, which was unreasonable in an institution which was trying to improve conditions.
Mr Burns altered the ruling to 8.00pm. Of course, there were
always inmates who preferred to go to bed immediately after
tea. (In my experience of being in charge of a residential
home, there were always residents who preferred to retire early,
even when there was a concert or social evening arranged.
Nothing would persuade them to stay up later!)

Back in 1931, middle-aged inmates were working in the laundry.
Most were around 60 years, but one lady was 70. She enjoyed
working and said it was something to do. They were up at
6.45am, with breakfast at 7.30am and in the laundry at 8.00am.
For this they were paid 6/7½d per week which, it must be
remembered, was spending money only; everything else was
provided. The wage for employed women from outside was 35/-
per week. While some of the female inmates were busy doing
jobs around the Workhouse, there were a few men who started
playing cards. Most of the Committee supported the Master when
he stopped the card games because of the dangers of gambling.
Money had mysteriously become available to gamble with, and it
was wiser to 'nip it in the bud'.

In August 1931 it was decided to lift the ban, temporarily, on
nursing staff marrying whilst working. It was to be tried for
three months and then reviewed. The fact that staff were being
allowed to get married, albeit a trial, was a step in the right
direction.

Because the Old
Lodge was too
small, Father ob-
tained permission
to move to the old
infectious diseases
hospital. This
building was much
more spacious, with
a closed verandah
along its length –
an ideal place to
play! It was also
near the bowling

*The author's grand-
mother and 'Jumbo'
outside the Engin-
eer's second resid-
ence (old Isolation
Block) in 1934. The
building is now
the Bolton College
of Nursing.*

green, another place to play around. My school friends sometimes came to play, but at first I had to ask permission for them to come into the grounds.

The Old Lodge became the residence for a succession of Assistant Matrons, the last one being Miss K M Cooper MBE, who afterwards became Matron of Bridgewater Hospital in Eccles. The very first Assistant Matron to Mr and Mrs Burns, in January 1935, was Miss Smith, who came from a large institution in London.

In 1935 the original mortuary building was demolished; a new one was built on the site of an old tool shed. This is the present-day mortuary, which has been extended in recent years.

Another improvement in Fishpool was the installation of new wireless sets in all the day rooms. In an effort to economise, old loudspeakers were used and these were no good at all when connected with the new sets. So the Public Assistance Committee agreed to new speakers being bought from Proffitt's radio shop in Bolton.

In 1934 the situation regarding mental patients was desperate. Acute psychiatric patients were being looked after on the 'Mental Block', alongside chronic sick mental inmates. They could not be transferred to other mental hospitals such as Prestwich, as they too were full. To help in the care of these patients, two additional male attendants were appointed, together with a temporary female attendant, Mrs Sawyer. On the mental wards (now Russell Vickers) Mr and Mrs Doherty were in charge of the Male and Female sides respectively. Their two daughters, Jean and Eileen, and I always went to the Boxing Day celebrations on the wards. We had a wonderful time, talking to and singing along with the inmates.

There was a lot to eat, and I particularly remember helping to give out shiny red apples and oranges to everyone. These inmates, in the ordinary way, did not have much to look forward to. With doors locked and barred, and with doors securing the side door top to bottom, any change in routine was welcome. They looked forward most to going across to the main hall whenever there was a concert. They walked across in crocodile file with attendants guiding them, the women in grey plaid shawls over striped dresses and men in grey flannel suits. They enjoyed joining in the fun, particularly the choruses. One little lady called 'Bobbie' sang louder than anyone else. The staff concerts were of particular interest to these ladies and gentlemen because one of their attendants, Mr Tony Enwright, was a fine tenor and used to sing songs like 'You are my Heart's Delight'. Mr Enwright worked as a male attendant from 1923 to 1947.

For their Christmas outing, in January 1935, 50 inmates enjoyed a visit to the circus at the Grand Theatre, Churchgate. Buses were hired from Bolton Corporation to take them, paid for from an Amenities Fund.

Early in 1935 Mrs Scholes, the laundress, retired and was succeeded by her assistant, Miss Pennington. By 1935 buses had started to operate to Townleys gate, running between there and Barrow Bridge. At that time all these buses were single deck, so that they could pass under the railway bridge and turn round inside the gates.

Minerva Road was then a private road to Fishpool and Townleys, the property of the Public Assistance Committee. New houses were built so that their back gardens faced Minerva Road, which was then fenced off. In 1935 it was found that some occupants of the new houses had put gates in their garden fences and were in the habit of climbing over the private fence to take a short cut to the new bus terminus, and one could not blame them!

Attached to the lodge office at the main gate is a small house, in which all the Assistant Masters have lived over the years. The first one to make use of the house, in 1935, was Mr James Haythornthwaite, who was promoted from being book-keeper. His wife was the Labour Mistress, responsible for female working inmates. Because their surname was so long they were known to

*The view from Fishpool Tower in the 1930s, looking towards Plodder Lane*

the staff as Mr and Mrs James. the last Deputy Superintendent to live there was Mr Frank Barratt, who was appointed Superintendent at Bridgewater Hospital, Eccles, in 1959.

The piggeries, situated where the Lady Tonge School is now, were a problem at this time. Pigs were normally sent to market for slaughtering, but a few became ill with pneumonia and had to be replaced when they died. Some were bought from Whittingham Hospital Farm for 13 guineas each. In 1936 rats were causing a nuisance around the piggeries. Nothing seemed to work to rid the buildings of them, so rat-catchers with ferrets were brought in. As our house was then near the piggeries, I remember the men putting the ferrets down into the drains and prepared holes, and the ferrets coming up with rats, or chasing them out of the holes. The men then put the dead rats in the bags which they carried.

I was quite friendly with one of the working inmates who looked after the donkey that pulled the cart used for the children's outings. In his spare time he looked after the bone shed, which was situated at the corner of the field opposite the present L Block. These bones came from the kitchens after the preparation of meat. The inmate's job was to keep the shed tidy and as clean as possible, as the smell of bones is not easy to forget! These bones were sold to a dealer, for a good price, and he used them to make glue. Scrap iron and bottles were also sold to make a bit of extra money for institution funds.

# Modernisation and other Changes

Mr and Mrs Burns retired from their posts as Master and Matron in 1935. Probably because they had been subservient first to the Guardians and then to the Public Assistance Committee, changes had been slow. But Mr and Mrs Taylor, the new Master and Matron who commenced duties on 4th June 1935, were a young, enthusiastic couple. They persuaded the Committee to implement many changes to improve the quality of life for the residents of the institution. Matron Taylor was Welsh, and coincidentally or otherwise, possessed a Welsh Corgi dog, which got used to wandering around the grounds.

In May 1935 Miss Kendrick, the cook, retired and was succeeded by Miss Stewart, whose sister was the staff cook. Both stayed for quite a few years. On 5th September two stalwarts of both Townleys and Fishpool were married: Mr Brislee, who had been the radiographer since the opening of the X-Ray department, and Miss Bella Ball, a senior clerk in the office at Fishpool.

Mr and Mrs Burns had started parties for the staff, although these had only been held at Christmas time. I remember very well Mr Burns 'letting his hair down' and dancing the polka with one of the attendants. Mr and Mrs Taylor, however, saw the need for a better social life for staff. The attendants and other staff worked long hours, and whist drives and dances throughout the year were much appreciated.

Mr Taylor instituted the visit of a dentist to the various wards, so that people who had been without dentures could have them. There was also an extra allowance of tobacco for male inmates doing work in the kitchens. Cinema shows were brought to inmates who could not go out. Those who could manage to go outside had weekly passes to visit the Ritz in Farnworth; four were allowed at a time. A library was set up, with books and magazines donated by local libraries and individuals.

Working inmates were rewarded in other ways. For instance, in May 1936 Alderman Warburton gave 31 tickets for the Bolton Wanderers versus Arsenal match at Burnden Park. There were also a few tickets available for each home game throughout the soccer season.

Large scale Christmas concerts, given by the staff, were started by Mr and Mrs Taylor in 1935; they were great fun and enjoyed by the inmates. There had been occasions in the past when nurses had formed a chorus in concerts presented by visiting artistes, but nothing on a large scale had been tried before. In the first year I took part in the concert by reciting a poem. The Master and Matron were great entertainers and sang comic songs such as 'I'm Shy, Mary Ellen, I'm Shy'. Mr Enwright was still singing, and Mr F Batty, a senior maintenance man, made a grand comedian.

That Christmas, more gifts came in from outside bodies than in previous years. Girls from Folds Road School gave woollen garments, knitted by themselves. Toys for the children were donated by Miss Rowntree of Chorley New Road and Alderman Mrs Lawson.

In December 1935 Walter Rushton, my grandfather, retired and my father was appointed Engineer in Charge. He remained in that post until he retired in 1962.

The total number of inmates on 7th March 1936 was 433, in the following categories:

|  | Men | Women | Infants |
|---|---|---|---|
| Over 70 years | 17 | 26 | |
| Under 70 years | 98 | 73 | |
| Receiving ward | 1 | 1 | |
| Mental wards | 65 | 59 | |
| Sick wards | 31 | 42 | |
|  | 212 | 201 | 20 |

At this stage there were still a lot of active men and women under 70 years old employed in various jobs around the institution. This was accepted as normal routine, but might have been seen as cheap labour by some. Women inmates helping in the laundry were greatly appreciated, because the amount of washing was increasing, with 500 patients at Townleys and 433 inmates at Fishpool. On average, 35,984 articles were washed each week.

Another bowling green for inmates was completed in front of what is now L 4. The original bowling green, laid near the present College of Nursing, was also used by staff for their competitions. For years two stone effigies stood on either side of the spectators' seat. Their origin is not known, but they currently reside within the College of Nursing building. Another innovation for staff social life was the building of tennis courts on the area that is now rough land next to Dowling Ward, and opposite the maintenance workshops. They were laid by Compsty & Son of Bolton at a cost of £62.

On 4th April 1936 the Rev Townsend of St James's, New Bury, was appointed Chaplain to Fishpool and Townleys. This was quite a heavy task, and he was assisted by Rev Weston, his Curate. Services of all denominations were still being held in the dining hall. The organ in the balcony had gone, and now there was a large pipe organ in the corner of the hall. Miss Edith Dunion had been the official organist for the services since 1920. She played for the Church of England and Nonconformist services on Sunday, with one of the inmates acting as organ blower. (The air was pumped to the organ by means of a large wooden lever.)

Miss Dunion had a young assistant organist to help her from 1922. This young lady was then ten years old, and her name was Edith Pepper. In addition to playing the organ, each May Miss Dunion and Edith brought children from St Barnabas Church, Bolton, to entertain the inmates with their Maypole and dance routines. Before there was a bus service, the two young ladies brought their charges on the tram to Great Lever and walked down the ginnel to Fishpool, often carrying storm lamps to light their journey home after the concert.

In 1936 Miss Dunion introduced the Crowning of the May Queen to the Maypole entertainment. This was a spectacular affair, with the inmates seated all round the dining hall and Master and Matron in draped armchairs at the centre of the circle. The May Queen and her retinue processed round and presented Matron Taylor with a bouquet. There then followed the Maypole dances. (It was at this particular event that I made up my mind that I, too, would be a Matron one day! Many years later this ambition was realised, when I was appointed Matron of an establishment in Stow-on-the-Wold, following a period when I had supervised residents at concerts.)

To return to Edith Pepper. She played the piano for the dancing and May Queen procession, and carried on helping Miss Dunion for many years. Edith is now Mrs Bentley, and is still doing voluntary work in the Department of Geriatrics at Bolton General for the WRVS. She also plays the organ (now an electronic portable) for services on the wards. Every Monday morning she is to be seen at the refreshment trolley in the Out-Patients' Department of Bolton Royal Infirmary on WRVS duty.

By August 1936 the main kitchens had been improved. The old fashioned gulleys, through which waste water had passed into the drains, were removed and replaced by new waste pipes. At the same time the patients' diet was improved and more variety provided. Improvements were also made to the nurses' and officers' rooms, and new bathrooms were installed. Most of these rooms were in 'The Tower', the present L1 and L2 wards and former Ridgeway, Rowlands and Kinlay wards.

Mr Taylor began the conversion of the large day rooms into smaller lounges. This was a major improvement for the residents, making life more comfortable and homely.

In 1937 Matron Taylor arranged some meetings of the Bolton branch of the Royal College of Nursing, of which she was a member, at Fishpool. As well as being a good place to have a group of nurses meeting together, it also helped to close the gap between nurses working in other fields and nurses in institutional care. The nurses from outside were able to see how circumstances had been improved for the residents.

May 1937 saw the Coronation of King George VI and Queen Elizabeth. There was entertainment, games and extra food for

St Barnabas May Queen and dance troupe in the 1950s. Mrs E Bentley, pianist, is on the extreme left. The girl seventh from the right on the front row is now Mrs A Taylor MP

(Courtesy Mrs E Bentley)

the residents and an extra day's leave, or pay of 12/6d, for the staff. Other improvements in 1937 included regular trips to the Gem and Queens cinemas in Bolton. Biscuits were introduced to go with the mid-morning drink: two biscuits per resident, or $\frac{2}{3}$ ounce, which was just under 5 ounces per week, the total cost being £275 per year.

Matron Taylor was anxious to encourage the older lady residents who were not working to make things like dishcloths, woollen bootees and socks for children. The staff had to be most diplomatic in trying to get them to do this as the women thought they were being made to do part-time work, and did not realise that it was occupational therapy, and therefore more for their benefit than anyone else's. More ambitious work was planned, but the scheme was not successful.

In October 1937 the balcony which ran the whole width at the back of the dining hall was removed. A permanent stage was built and professionally fitted with lighting and rust-coloured velvet curtains. Later on, matching curtains were fitted to the windows. A new floor was laid, and the whole room tastefully decorated (with wallpaper, for the first time). While these alterations were being carried out, special arrangements were made for the day rooms to be converted into lounges with dining facilities and a temporary chapel was constructed in one of the lounges.

Towards the end of 1937 the number of chronic sick was increasing. Infirm 2 (Dowling Ward) then had 58 patients, the majority of whom had been transferred from Townleys Hospital. These patients were nursed most diligently by a dedicated staff, supervised by one sister. There were 26 children in the nursery; the female mental ward and the observation and sick wards in that department were constantly full, as was the male side.

In December 1937 a male attendant on the mental block requested permission to take a mental patient to a football match at Burnden Park occasionally. This was refused by the Public Assistance Committee, either because they thought it unwise at that time for staff to get too involved with patients, or because of safety considerations for both patient and surrounding spectators. Something that was approved was Mr and Mrs Taylor's suggestion that staff go round all the wards on Christmas Eve, singing carols. Also new was a social evening for all active residents and staff on Christmas Night. The usual Christmas fare was served on Boxing Day. There were visits from civic dignitaries as in previous years, and these councillors and members of the Committee saw a transformed dining hall.

Early in 1938 spare land at the back of the mental block (now the site of the McKay Clinic and psychiatric day hospital) was fenced off and made into a garden and exercise area for patients. This was favourably commented upon by a Government Inspector; he also gave a favourable report on the way the

# Dietary Tables for Inmates of the Sick Wards and Mental Wards and Infants at the Fishpool Institution.

**DINNER.**

**First Day.**

| | |
|---|---|
| Roast Beef .. .. .. | 3 ozs. |
| Potatoes .. .. .. .. | 6 ozs. |
| Peas .. .. .. .. | 4 ozs. |
| Bread .. .. .. .. | 4 ozs. |
| Pudding .. .. .. .. | 6 ozs. |

**Second Day.**

| | |
|---|---|
| Boiled Bacon .. .. .. | 3 ozs. |
| Potatoes .. .. .. .. | 6 ozs. |
| Beans .. .. .. .. | 4 ozs. |
| Bread .. .. .. .. | 4 ozs. |

**Third Day.**

| | |
|---|---|
| Soup .. .. .. .. | 1 pint. |
| Bread .. .. .. .. | 4 ozs. |
| Pudding .. .. .. .. | 8 ozs. |

**Fourth Day.**

| | |
|---|---|
| Meat & Potato Pie.. .. | 16 ozs. |
| Bread .. .. .. .. | 4 ozs. |
| Tea .. .. .. .. .. | $\frac{1}{2}$ pint. |

**Fifth Day.**

| | |
|---|---|
| Sausages .. .. .. | 4 ozs. |
| Mashed Potatoes .. .. | 6 ozs. |
| Bread .. .. .. .. | 4 ozs. |
| Pudding .. .. .. .. | 6 ozs. |

**Sixth Day.**

| | |
|---|---|
| Boiled Beef .. .. .. | 3 ozs. |
| Potatoes .. .. .. .. | 6 ozs. |
| Cabbage, Turnips or Carrots .. .. | 4 ozs. |
| Bread .. .. .. .. | 4 ozs. |

**Seventh Day.**

| | |
|---|---|
| Cold Beef with Pickles or Sauce .. .. | 3 ozs. |
| Potatoes .. .. .. .. | 6 ozs. |
| Pudding .. .. .. .. | 6 ozs. |
| Bread .. .. .. .. | 4 ozs. |

**TEA.**

| | |
|---|---|
| Tea .. .. .. .. .. .. .. .. .. | 1 pint. |
| Bread .. .. .. .. .. .. .. .. | 6 ozs. |
| Butter .. .. .. .. .. .. .. .. | $\frac{1}{2}$ oz. |

On each of four days in the week one of the following items to be given in addition, viz.:—

| | |
|---|---|
| Stewed Prunes .. .. .. .. .. | 3 ozs. |
| Fish Cake .. .. .. .. .. .. | 1 |
| Cake, Tea Cake .. .. .. .. .. | 2 ozs. |
| Tripe .. .. .. .. .. .. .. | 3 ozs. |
| Green Salad (when in season). | |

**NOTE.**—Inmates are to receive rations according to appetite provided that the allowances shall in no case exceed the amounts set forth in these Dietary Tables.

*Extract from inmates' dietary tables, 1936*
*(Courtesy Mr S Eccles, Catering Officer)*

wards on the block were run. One thing still not going well was occupational work. Residents were reluctant to try new things. The decision to employ a part-time teacher, and to form smaller groups, was deferred for the time being.

In February 1938 a new Assistant Master, Mr Huggett, began duties. He and his wife lived in at the Lodge House, and apart from war service in the RAF, he stayed in his post for a few years.

In February, too, St Bedes children and adults gave a performance of a show called 'All for a Shilling a Day'. The large audience, including 40 patients who were brought across from Townleys, and children from Hollins Cottage Homes, enjoyed the show. Between then and May there were four concert parties to entertain the residents and groups and individuals gave their services freely to cheer both the permanent residents of Fishpool (who were in the majority) and patients in Townleys. Fund raising here was not necessary, although Bolton Royal Infirmary depended upon voluntary contributions at that time. To this day, the people of Bolton take a great interest in Townleys and the tradition of generosity has continued.

Towards the end of 1938 Mr Taylor decided that it was time to consider more full-time paid workers for manual jobs around the institution and its grounds. Over the preceding few years the number of male residents under 70 years old had decreased, so there were not many able to cope with the various jobs. The number of women residents who worked in the sewing room was also declining, and some younger residents were discharging themselves, determined to try and cope on their own outside the institution.

In August 1938 preparations for war were discussed: ARP schemes, gas mask issues, a decontamination centre, air raid shelters and a fire engine based at Fishpool. From the beginning of 1939, ARP training for staff commenced, with fire drill, bomb disposal demonstrations and experimental black-outs.

At Christmas, the staff concert was performed for the first time on the new stage. I was given the honour of 'guesting' at one or two of these annual concerts, introduced as, 'The Engineer's daughter, who will now give us a song'.

# Wartime

In between the preparations for the inevitable war, routine caring duties continued. Concert parties visited as usual, and Matron Taylor and her staff succeeded in encouraging the younger residents to knit shawls for the older ladies, to make dish cloths and learn how to do embroidery. Meanwhile, some of the workmen who were reservists were given leave from Fishpool and Townleys to take their Forces training. Black-out curtains and blinds were ordered, and mattresses with bedsteads were put in the cellars in readiness for air-raids. The team of Auxiliary Firemen was strengthened.

The black-out material was put to use in the August. 900 yards were used for day rooms, bedrooms and sick wards. The dining room windows needed special attention because of their size. The new velvet curtains were quite heavy, but still had to be lined with the black material.

Sixty-eight extra beds were put into some of the day rooms, anticipating the need to move patients or accommodate casualties – in short, ready for anything. Facilities were made available for a further 50 beds and 82 Townleys patients were transferred over to Fishpool to make room in the wards for casualties or sick soldiers. All this required extra staff, and both Townleys and Fishpool personnel pulled hard together. Everyone worked extra hours to get the job done – off duty time was not even considered, and annual leave in a lot of cases was suspended.

A proposed new building scheme was postponed indefinitely and the land was cultivated instead. A large patch of land fronting the College of Nursing was also cultivated for growing vegetables. This space is now a car park.

In spite of all the troubles, the staff concert went ahead on Boxing Day 1939. The Auxiliary Fire Service members also gave

*The Duck Pond, now drained and grassed over, with Hollins Cottage Homes in the background in the early 1940s*

a concert in the Christmas period. For the first time, concerts were relayed through speakers to the residents on the chronic sick wards, and this gave tremendous pleasure to all. Later on, in April 1940, Sunday Services were broadcast as well.

The Chaplain, Mr Townsend, arranged for people at St James's, New Bury, to make up 100 parcels for patients and residents who had no relatives. These were distributed by parishioners and Mr Townsend himself, who was a very popular figure around Fishpool. He did not have a car and was regularly to be seen riding his bicycle from the vicarage in Highfield Road and down the ginnel alongside the railway to the gates of the institution.

The weather in January 1940 was severe. Heavy snows occurred, with drifts of eighteen inches to two feet deep everywhere. Some in the hospital grounds were four and five feet deep. This intensely cold weather brought extra work on all the staff. Labourers tried to clear the roads, maintenance men continually repaired burst pipes, and nurses were kept busy treating patients who had developed chesty colds. 45 residents had their chests rubbed with camphorated oil every night – an old fashioned, tried and tested remedy.

To help with the labour shortage, men on outdoor relief in Bolton were given proper work at Fishpool and Townleys. There was much to be done – work on the cultivated land under the supervision of the foreman, Mr Southern, the general upkeep of buildings and grounds, and the care of the pigs and piggeries. These were on the same land as many years earlier, the present site of Lady Tonge School. Although the pigs came under the Ministry of Food regulations during the war, some were still killed for consumption in the institution at Christmas time. Labourers were employed to remove the railings which surrounded the gardens (now the site of the car park and Day Hospital at the back of Dowling Block) and these railings were used as scrap metal for the war effort.

By July 1940, residents capable of walking were moved to the air-raid shelters; a large shelter had been built in one of the yards and another on spare land. There were also beds in the cellars for a few inmates and staff. Moving confused and frightened residents presented quite a problem when the air-raid warnings came. One advantage was that the staff had more time than the general public, because Fishpool and Townleys received the two earlier 'purple' and 'red' warnings before the sirens sounded. These were relayed by telephone to the ARP post, and I remember them also being telephoned to our house, when Father would depart immediately to the wardens' post at the hospital. At the same time, Mother and I would hurry to the cellars along with the others, and stay there until the 'All Clear' sounded. The Chaplain always came to comfort the frightened residents during the air-raids.

My mother 'did her bit' by joining the Civil Nursing Reserve.

She passed First Aid and Home Nursing examinations, and then helped on the wards at Townleys, along with many other ladies who until then had had time on their hands. This VAD work led a few younger women to go on to general training and qualify as State Registered Nurses.

In March 1940 my father was offered the part-time post of Engineer at Hulton Lane Hospital, in addition to his appointment as Engineer to Townleys and Fishpool. For this extra responsibility his salary was increased to £312 per year.

In October, fifty chronic sick women evacuees from London hospitals were sent to the institution. Matron Holland at Townleys provided some of her nurses to meet the train at London Road Station, Manchester, and a convoy of ambulances brought the patients to Bolton. Nurses at Fishpool remained on duty for 35 hours, waiting to receive the Londoners, because the trains were late. The staff also stayed on duty to settle the patients in their new surroundings. They were suffering from fatigue and shock, and in addition needed a lot of cleaning up to be made comfortable.

Later on, Mr Townsend was to the fore, organising ladies from the Church to visit the evacuees and 'adopt them'. Roman Catholic priests and Free Church ministers also visited regularly. Relatives of the evacuee patients were also looked after. Local people offered them accommodation and train tickets were paid for by charitable organisations. Many of the relatives had lost everying in the London air-raids, and they needed, and were given, a lot of help from the people of Bolton.

All the office staff were called up into the Forces, as were two young working residents, depriving the storekeeper and baker of assistants. For the first time in many years there was no staff concert at Christ-

*Matron Hilda Bethel. Before coming to Townleys she was Deputy Matron at Redhill County Hospital, Middlesex, for six years*

mas and instead the 'Joy Boys' concert party obliged. Nurses arranged parties on the wards during the afternoons, and on Christmas morning directors and staff from Walker's Tannery in Thynne Street came to the institution with gifts of 540 meat pies, assorted pastries and the sum of 22/6d. The visitors were taken round all the wards and were impressed by what they saw. Apparently they had been told that Fishpool was like a 'second Pentonville Prison'! This Christmas visit with gifts became a regular occurrence for a few years following that first kind thought.

Hope Hospital in Salford was bombed, the Medical Superintendent and Matron were killed, and at the beginning of 1941 some patients were transferred to Fishpool. Hope laundry had suffered in the bombing and machinery had broken down. Fishpool laundry took some of their washing - 611 blankets and 96 towels in the first instance. The cost of this was met by the Salford authority.

Owing to the shortage in staff it was difficult to cope with casuals, and with the mental patients who were sometimes admitted as emergencies during the night. Active casuals were turned away and only those who were too frail to carry on, or were in a poor physical condition, were admitted for the night.

More London hospital patients arrived and the number from Hope Hospital was also increasing. Sick residents at Fishpool were transferred to a special ward there instead of being transferred to Townleys. Civil Nursing Reserve staff were employed at Townleys and Fishpool to complement the regular staff. The CNR members got £1 rations allowance whilst on leave, and ordinary staff were paid only 15/-. This caused quite a lot of resentment among the permanent staff, and eventually they were paid the same amount.

In June 1941 I had left school (Mount St Joseph's, Deane) and commenced nursing at Wrightington Hospital near Wigan. At that time Wrightington was for the treatment of orthopaedic tuberculosis. There were a few hut-type wards for pulmonary tuberculosis, but 17-year-old probationer nurses were not allowed on these wards. The orthopaedic patients were very long term - one to two years on plaster beds, or frames - so we got to know them very well. In spite of this, as soon as I was eighteen I started general training at Townleys. Even though I had a home in the grounds, Matron Bethel suggested that I live in the Nurses' Home for the first three months. (Matron Holland had retired.)

The growing of salads, vegetables and oats as part of the war effort was so successful at Fishpool that, in addition to supplying the hospital, food was supplied to the London evacuees and their helpers who were housed at Flash Street School. The oats were grown mainly as a result of help given by the Bolton Parks Department, but most of the work was done by Mr

Southern, the foreman gardener, and his staff. In September 1941 a Harvest Festival was held in the dining hall and the proceeds from the collection were used to buy silver candlesticks and vases for the altar.

Ways of raising funds for the war effort were devised. One of the staff, Sister Hall, arranged beetle drives for the Forces' Comforts Fund. There were collections from all departments for the Red Cross Fund. All residents were keen to contribute and raised about 18/- per month. About £5 was raised each month by these collections.

Though everything seemed to be going smoothly, there was an acute shortage of beds for Bolton people, so the remaining patients from London and Salford were transferred to other hospitals; some went to the Fylde coast and some to Birch Hill, Rochdale.

It was at this time that a nurse from the Channel Islands made her home at Fishpool. Miss Le Pelly, an assistant attendant, managed to get away to England before the German occupation

*Mr Rushton (Engineer) and Mr Southern (Gardener) outside the original Boilerhouse and Laundry. A new Boilerhouse was built on this land in 1966*

and obtained work at the institution. I think she settled down in Bolton afterwards.

In February 1942 the Civil Defence members arranged a concert for the residents. Entertainers included the Gorse Brothers, Miss Marion Isherwood and Mr J Ince. The Gorse Brothers became well known nationally. Hylda Baker also used to come and entertain in her early days, as she was a local girl.

In 1942 there were only 76 ambulant men in the institution, and only a few of these were able to do heavy work. The numbers were:

|  | Men | Women |  |
|---|---|---|---|
| Over 70 years | 38 | 35 |  |
| Under 70 years | 38 | 63 |  |
| Mental wards | 62 | 53 |  |
| Frail elderly | 85 | 49 |  |
| Chronic sick |  | 88 | Total 511 |

Maintenance work was getting heavier for the staff. In one month the engineers spent:
  264½ hours on structural work
  158¾ hours on repairs in laundry
  32 hours on boilers
  208¾ hours at Townleys Hospital
  120½ hours at Hollins Cottage Homes

The joiners worked:
  77½ hours on repair of furniture at Fishpool
  131 hours in general repairs at Fishpool
  308 hours at Townleys Hospital
  147½ hours at Hollins Cottage Homes

In April 1942 the hot water system failed completely. The maintenance staff worked together under my father to replace the blocked pipes. The clerk to the Public Assistance Committee wrote to my father afterwards and complimented everyone on working so efficiently to get the central heating and the hot water on again quickly.

In this year we moved from the bungalow to the house that had previously been the Assistant Medical Officer's residence, almost next to the bungalow. The house had been vacated by Mr Farrell and his family on his retirement from the post of Hospital Steward at Townleys. It was a change for us to live in a normal house after the unusual bungalow, even though it was situated between the piggeries and the duck pond. My parents remained there until my father's retirement in 1962.

During Bolton Holiday Week of 1942 the staff arranged an outing to Moss Bank Park for residents. This was to be a regular occurrence – at least until the end of the war, when more ambitious outings would be arranged. 80 residents enjoyed an afternoon out in pleasant surroundings, with tea provided. There were other pleasant events, such as when Mr Almond of the wholesale market gave 84 boxes of strawberries to Fishpool. These were divided between the institution, Townleys and Hollins Cottages. Bolton Home Guard personnel gave a concert, along with their band. Residents and staff took part in a National Day of Prayer, in common with churches throughout the country.

Mr Taylor arranged for the men to have fireside chairs in their day rooms. I am sure that this gesture was greatly appreciated, as previously they had had the bentwood type of armchair. The day rooms were also improved by being washed and painted in brighter colours. One of the things that people remembered about the Workhouse in years past was the dark green and brown paint on corridors and in day rooms. The bright paint was not only pleasant for residents and patients, but made for better and more cheerful working conditions for the staff.

About 1942 the name 'attendant' for nurses was abolished, and they became known as assistant nurses, and began to be officially recognised as such. When the inspectors from the Board of Control visited in December that year they were impressed with the improvements and with the new status for nurses.

In April 1943 a new 'air-speed drier' was installed in the laundry. It was more economical on steam and consequently there was a saving on the coal bill of £7/15s per week. This was just as well, because the number of articles being washed by July was 43,000 weekly. There were 34 workers with, for the first time, two men on the large washing machines.

Patients on the mental wards were not left out of the general improvements. Easy chairs were put in their day rooms and two cabinet gramophones, with a supply of records, were installed.

Amongst other things, the ladies of the Women's Voluntary Service gave 28 hot water bottles for use by some of the residents of Fishpool and Townleys. (This organisation had been launched in 1938, in preparation for the war.) In 1944 clothing and bedroom slippers were distributed, but the Women's Voluntary Service did not visit officially until 1956, when the trolley shops were organised by Mrs E Warr, Mrs W Wadsworth and Mrs M Rushton.

Mr Ernest Clarke, who had served as the institution's barber since 1906, retired in November 1944. He had been a respected employee and very popular amongst the staff. His son, Ellis, was a Bolton councillor for twenty years, and both his grandsons served as Mayor. Mr Powell succeeded Mr Clarke as barber at Fishpool, and Mr Billington, son of the former Public Hangman, was the Townleys Hospital barber.

Social activities for staff continued to improve, and due to the efforts of Mr Taylor a staff dance was arranged in March 1944. It was an occasion to help raise money for the Mayor's Fund, and at the same time gave the majority of staff a pleasant respite.

All beds at Townleys were full at this time. Wounded and sick British soldiers had arrived, as also had some German prisoners. The Germans were on C 3 Ward, under the care of Sister Porter. I was working on this ward then, and the prisoners were given the same nursing care as other patients. No privileges were allowed, although Red Cross Parcels arrived from time to time. There was always a British soldier on guard at the ward door, but sometimes it was difficult to control the high spirits of the German soldiers who were recovering. Richard Greene, the actor appearing in 'Desert Rats' at the Theatre Royal, visited the British soldiers to boost their morale whilst in hospital. The bowling greens and billiards room were made available to the convalescing British soldiers, who found them a welcome change from the wards, or just walking about the grounds.

Accommodation for the chronic sick was short. Fishpool staff nursed patients in some of their dormitories, particularly as the number of ambulant residents was falling.

The Maypole festival from St Barnabas Church and the Slatersfield Sermons came in 1944. These two events in particular had become traditional over the years; St Barnabas children also started a Sunday 'afternoon sing' round the wards.

1944 saw the deaths of the Rev Townsend, who had done such good work, and Mr Taylor, the Master, who had done much to improve conditions and tried to abolish the 'workhouse' image. Mr Townsend was succeeded by the Rev H Fielding, who in later years became Vicar of Bolton, and then the Venerable Archdeacon of Rochdale. At this time the Roman Catholic Chaplain also retired and Father Mahoney was appointed in a temporary post.

On the death of Mr Taylor, Mr and Mrs Burns, the previous Master and Matron, were called out of retirement to run the institution until a new joint appointment was made. Mrs Taylor obtained a single post as Matron of Whitecross Hospital in Warrington.

# The Greatest Improvements for the Quality of Life

The Burns' stayed until January 1945, when the new Master and Matron, Mr and Mrs D Ernsting, arrived. Mr Ernsting wasted no time in continuing the improvements, such as installing heating in the bathrooms of the sick wards and lowering the ceilings to conserve heat. He also considerably improved the diet of both residents and patients. Alternatives to the basic three meals were introduced, such as sausage or cold meat for breakfast, rabbit for lunch and cheese and fruit as alternatives to other puddings. For tea, there was meat or fish paste and baked custard and jam. Subject to supplies being available, supper at 7.30pm was introduced. Tea, coffee or soup was available with bread and butter and biscuits. Considering that the war was still on, this was a very good diet, with all the essential nutrients.

Problems arose for porters at the lodge office and gates. The gate porter had to keep a record of staff as they passed through the turnstile to go on and off duty, and the telephone switchboard, still housed in the lodge, was coping with an increasing number of calls. The porters' other duties included assisting with the removal of bodies to the mortuary and issuing clothing to residents as they were admitted. A young man was appointed to operate the switchboard and this helped; he dealt with an average of 410 incoming, 230 outgoing and 600 internal calls daily. To ease the task of checking employees in and out, the turnstile was removed and a time clock put in its place on Mr Ernsting's recommendation. The disappearance of the turnstile was a step in the right direction, away from the locked-up

*Presentation of medals, 1946. Standing: Dr E S Gawne (Medical Superintendent), Mrs H Bethel (Matron), M Warburton, E Rushton (Connor), L Eastwood, M Stevens, Sister Rollinson (Tutor), D Atherton, N Massaur, Nurse Worrall, Nurse Tansey, E Patterson, Sister Greaves (Deputy Tutor), N Kay, J Crump, M McKinlay, Mayoress S Rigby. Sitting: A Wilson, J Sharples, M Purtell, M Quinn, T Tansey, A Buxton, M Moylan, S Vause.*

appearance of the Workhouse. The removal of the lodge gates later on made the transformation of the entrance complete.

Time saving equipment, such as a bread cutting and buttering machine and plate washing machines, was installed in Townleys and Fishpool kitchens. A new extension for extra toilets and bathrooms was built at the end of the male block (L 4), which must have been a welcome improvement for all.

In May 1945 a night sister (Sister Monk) was appointed at Fishpool for the first time, although there was a shortage of nurses on the sick wards during the day. To resolve this, Matron Ernsting arranged with Matron Bethel to 'borrow' nurses temporarily from Townleys.

Matron Ernsting surveyed the position of women residents (and that of a few men) regarding occupational therapy. Out of 506 persons, including chronic sick and mental patients, 117 were able to do simple work. Of these, 86 said they would like to try diversional therapy. This was the beginning of the therapy that we see going on today on a larger scale: the garden cultivation by patients, painting, modelling, and so on. Occupational therapy was also started in the mental wards. There was rug making and raffia work and, in a garden at the back of the block, hens roamed and rabbits were housed in hutches. These interests provided a pleasant diversion for the mental patients of all ages.

May 8th 1945 was VE Day. There were parties, concerts and a pint of beer for those who wanted it. Over at Townleys, I was on night duty and had to cook egg and bacon breakfasts for the patients on E 2. Red, white and blue streamers were put up in all departments.

Later in the year, things were getting back to normal after the war and men were returning from the Forces and other work of national importance. However, as in 1918, there was a shortage of tradesmen. Building work all over the country was delayed, and so proposed alterations and extensions at Townleys and Fishpool were held up.

Activities for residents and patients continued and improved. The manager of the Odeon Cinema gave free tickets, the Lido Cinema in Bradshawgate also provided seats, and so did Burnden Park for the Bolton Wanderers matches. Concert parties continued to visit regularly. Leave for residents to go out of the institution was at that time restricted to one day per month. Mr Ernsting asked for, and got, permission to grant leave to residents at his discretion. The staff, too, were looked after by the Ernstings. Matron arranged for resident staff to have breakfast in bed on their days off, and mornings off duty.

In February 1946 the roads were resurfaced to facilitate the smooth running of food trolleys between the main kitchen and the wards. Male residents were no longer required to peel potatoes in the kitchens; two men were paid to do this chore.

Regular visits by an optician to check eyesight and supply spectacles to residents were instituted by Mr Ernsting in 1946. A survey of 450 residents revealed that 171 would not be able to make use of spectacles because of their mental or physical condition. However, of the remaining 279 residents and patients, 173 would benefit. Thus Mr Ernsting made the pleasure of reading magazines and books possible for many. The then Member of Parliament, Mr John Lewis, referred the plan to the Ministry of Health, and Mr Aneurin Bevan (the Minister) was so impressed that he asked for an up-to-date report. Mr Bevan stated that he would consider what publicity could usefully be given to the scheme. From 5th July 1948 eyesight testing became the responsibility of the Regional Hospital Boards and Executive Councils under the National Health Act.

At this time there was a completely new innovation in care, and something which created a lot of publicity – the appointment of a hairdresser. A room was furnished as a salon where residents could have their hair styled or permed. 185 females benefitted from this, as did 66 children at Hollins Cottage Homes. (Younger children, by this time, had moved from Fishpool to the Homes.)

There was an acute shortage of nurses to work on chronic sick wards in post-war years. A recruitment exhibition was held in

*Members of the Staff Bowling Club, 1947. Mr Ernsting is third from the right on the front row; Alderman Mrs Reece (President) is seated in the centre.* *(Courtesy Mr D Ernsting)*

Bolton, where photographs of Fishpool wards were displayed and demonstrations of the work carried out were given. One interesting aspect of this was that a motor driver at Fishpool, who had been a sick berth attendant in the Royal Navy during the war, was persuaded by Mr Ernsting to make nursing his career. After qualifying as a State Registered Nurse, he became one of the first male staff nurses.

On 17th April 1946 the first staff canteen was opened. This was housed in the small block in front of Dowling Ward and was a great success. By the end of April it had served 624 dinners, 1,993 hot beverages and 340 teas. The takings for the period amounted to £40/12s.

Other improvements included the introduction of ward helps for serving meals and tidying the wards. The farm and gardens produced enough lettuce and cress to supply Townleys and the British Restaurant, which handled distribution to the schools feeding centre. Signalling points were installed to locate doctors. The laundry was dealing with 60,000 articles a week, mainly due to an increase in washing from Townleys Hospital, and four men were now employed for the heavy work. Later, extra calenders (to iron sheets) and a twin press were introduced. Hospital traffic on the road was increasing and a few staff now owned cars, so a speed limit of 10 miles per hour was introduced in the grounds.

Vagrants were once again causing problems. Since the end of the war 270 tramps had been admitted, of whom 30 were found to be verminous in one way or another and had to be cleaned up. During 1947 quite a few young men aged about 20 were admitted nightly. Mr Ernsting took the trouble to talk to them and persuaded them to enter the Wayfarers Hostel, Chilton Hall, Darlington. At the Hall they were rehabilitated to normal living and trained for a job. Tramps continued to be received into centres attached to institutions until the early 1960s, when the Department of Health and Social Security closed them and opened their own reception centres, which were very few compared with the number closed. However, the tramps did not go away, as it had been assumed they would. Places to sleep were few and, as a result, tramp shelters run by voluntary bodies, such as the ones 'under the arches' in Manchester, were opened.

Back in 1946, a horse and cart was still being used for duties such as the transporting of garden produce, manure and so on. One day the horse bolted through the grounds, smashing the cart beyond repair. Bolton Cleansing Department offered to lend a cart, and later offered to sell it to Fishpool for £20. On finding that this cart had dry rot, Mr Ernsting declined the offer and obtained a new one!

Interior-sprung mattresses were introduced for chronic sick patients - a long way from the straw mattresses used for the sick in the 1860s.

Letters of appreciation from grateful relatives were received quite frequently. On one chronic sick ward (now L 1) there were windows only on one side of the ward. Mr Ernsting had large mirrors put on the blank walls so that patients in beds with backs to the windows could see the reflection of Plodder Lane and even traffic going along the lane outside the grounds. This was a wonderful idea – it was certainly better than staring at blank walls.

1947 saw further improvements. A 'tuck shop' for residents was opened by Mr and Mrs Ernsting. Pictures were obtained from the Art Gallery, on loan, for the lounges, and were changed periodically. Blind residents were taken on outings and to socials organised by the Blind Society of Bolton.

Of course, there were still problems to overcome. Four men over 65 years were housed in the bungalow because of the shortage of beds in the main building. Residents who slept on the first floor of the main building had to climb up the stairs, because at that time lifts had not been installed.

As in the old days, the institution took in one or two homeless families from time to time. In May 1947 a couple and their children were admitted. However, unlike the old days, this man was allowed (indeed, encouraged) to go out to work. Co-operation between staff at Fishpool and welfare officers meant that some accommodation was found for the family. When help

*The Laundry, 1960. The elevated office at the back on the left was positioned so that the Laundress could observe all the workers*

had been given with furnishing a house, the family was able to leave Fishpool and move in.

In spite of efforts to make Fishpool homely and provide a free existence for residents, there was always the odd miscreant. Whilst on leave, one resident sold his overcoat (provided by the institution) to a man in a public house for 10/-. It was later recovered by the police. There was also the man who had his tobacco allowance withdrawn for two weeks when he returned from leave drunk and disorderly and assaulted another resident.

Early in 1948 it was necessary to employ more domestic staff because young working female residents were discharged outside. This was the beginning of the new era in the use of Fishpool as a hospital for the chronic sick. Fit elderly were gradually transferred to buildings which were adapted into comfortable homes, such as Watermillock and Smithills Hall. Experienced senior staff went with them. Having familiar faces around them in their new environment helped the residents to settle down very well.

The care of the elderly sick and remaining residents at Fishpool went on. Gifts continued to flow in for the wards: books, pictures, easy chairs and flowers were all given by people of

*Maintenance staff with the author's father (kneeling at front) on his retirement in 1962. Mr Harry Hawkins (extreme left, fourth row from front) was appointed his successor. Mr Tom Cooper (extreme left, third row from front) was the next Engineer until his retirement in 1985*

various organisations in Bolton. No doubt their actions were prompted by the enthusiasm of the Ernstings in making a well run, comfortable hospital.

At this time I was a Student Health Visitor in Manchester, and I was so impressed by the changes at Fishpool that I asked permission for my colleagues to visit the various departments. (It was part of a Health Visitor's training to visit a large residential establishment.) My tutor was so pleased with the visit that Fishpool became a model. There were annual visits by students and Mr and Mrs Ernsting lectured to each party.

On 5th July 1948 the National Health Service came into being. Names were changed: Fishpool became first Townleys Annexe and later Townleys Branch. Now, of course, the whole complex, Fishpool and Townleys, is the Bolton District General Hospital. Local people sometimes still use the old names – though with affection and, I am glad to say, without the old stigma.

The buildings may be old now, but the work of nursing care, rehabilitation and physiotherapy is second to none.

* * * * * *

# Acknowledgments

The author gratefully acknowledges the assistance, including the provision of documents and photographs, of the following:

Mr K Campbell, Archivist; Mr D Billington; Bolton District General Hospital (Department of Medical Illustration); Bolton Evening News; Bolton Reference Library; Farnworth Library; WEA (Local History Workshop); WRVS; Mrs E Bentley; Mrs Wolfendale; Ex-officers and employees of Townleys, especially Mr and Mrs D Ernsting, Mr F Barratt, Mr T Cooper, Miss Sally Gorringe and Miss O White.

Special thanks to my husband Bill for his help and support throughout the project.

---

Key to the plan: 1 Superintendent's House; 2 Stores; 3 Gymnasium; 4 Girls' Cottage Homes; 5 Hospital; 6 Boys' Cottage Homes; 7 Infectious Diseases Hospital; 8 Greenhouses; 9 Infirmary; 10 Piggeries; 11 Piggeries; 12 Stables; 13 Coach House; 14 Female Inmates' Clothing Store; 15 Committee Rooms; 16 Corn Grinding; 17 Main Buildings (Males); 18 Apartments of Master and Matron; 19 Main Buildings (Females); 20 Laundry; 21 Dining Hall; 22 Cook House; 23 Stores; 24 Hospital (Females); 25 Hospital (Males); 26 Chapel and Burial Ground; 27 Female Phthisical Hospital; 28 Female Hospital; 29 Medical Officer's Residence; 30 Male Hospitals; 31 Male Phthisical Hospital; 32 Porter's Lodge; 33 Probationary Ward; 34 Townleys Farm; 35 Nurses' Home; 36 Receiving Home for Boys and Girls. 37 Gate House.